973.752
MON

P9-BZS-350

Dear Martha

Letter to day

get it tomorro

LITTLE CREEK BRANCH

THE MONITOR CHRONICLES

One Sailor's Account

❖

Today's Campaign to Recover the Civil War Wreck

THE MARINERS' MUSEUM

EDITED BY WILLIAM MARVEL

SIMON & SCHUSTER

NEW YORK LONDON TORONTO SYDNEY SINGAPORE

ACW 5168
973. 752
(more)

SIMON & SCHUSTER
Rockefeller Center
1230 Avenue of the Americas
New York, NY 10020

Copyright © 2000 by The Mariners' Museum
All rights reserved,
including the right of reproduction
in whole or in part in any form.

SIMON & SCHUSTER and colophon are registered trademarks
of Simon & Schuster, Inc.

Designed by Sam Potts
Manufactured in the United States of America

1   3   5   7   9   10   8   6   4   2

Library of Congress Cataloging-in-Publication Data
The Monitor chronicles : one sailor's account : today's campaign to recover
the Civil War wreck / the Mariners' Museum ; edited by William Marvel.
p.   cm.
Historical text largely based on and including Civil War letters written by George Geer.
Includes bibliographical references (p.) and index.
1. Monitor (Ironclad) 2. Geer, George S.—Correspondence. 3. Sailors—United States—
Correspondence. 4. United States—History—Civil War, 1861–1865—Naval operations.
5. United States—History—Civil War, 1861–1865—Personal narratives. 6. Shipwrecks—
North Carolina—Hatteras, Cape. 7. Underwater archaeology—North Carolina—
Hatteras, Cape. 8. Excavations (Archaeology)—North Carolina—Hatteras, Cape.
I. Geer, George S. II. Marvel, William. III. Mariners' Museum (Newport News, Va.)

E595.M7 M655 2000
973.7'52—dc21   00-027158

ISBN 0-684-86997-7

CONTENTS

FOREWORD

————◆————

William C. Davis

PERHAPS NEVER IN HISTORY was a dramatic new weapon of war kept less a secret from the enemy. Almost from the moment its construction began in 1861, the USS *Monitor* attracted the attention of public and press alike. Not surprisingly, the Confederates kept a concerned eye on the progress of the revolutionary new ironclad warship, too, for they well knew it was being built largely to counter their own ersatz ironclad CSS *Virginia*, rebuilt on the hull of the old USS *Merrimack*. Indeed, rarely, if ever, has there been a meeting of two antagonists that seemed more fated from the beginning than the epic encounter on March 8, 1862, in Hampton Roads, Virginia, when for a few hours they gave each other their undivided attention and redirected the course of naval warfare for all time.

Sadly, the cranky *Virginia*, beset with all the problems that hasty construction and inadequate materials could impose, lived for only two months after their encounter before her own crew destroyed her to prevent capture. Though long remembered, she yet remains imperfectly understood because so little of her remains, not even a photograph. But her great foe, and by far the greater advance in technological innovation, has enjoyed a happier fate even though she, too, did not last out the year before going to the bottom of the sea off Cape Hatteras, North Carolina. We have photographs of the *Monitor*, and we have many of her builders' plans, shipyard models, and even woodcuts of her interior appointments. But most of all, we still have the *Monitor* herself. Found in the 1970s lying 200 feet beneath the waves where she sank in a gale, she was almost untouched until her rediscovery.

In August 1979, I had the rare opportunity to see the *Monitor* during the early research dives on the wreck carried out by the National Oceanic and Atmospheric Administration of the Department of Commerce. Aboard the four-man submersible *Johnson Sea Link II*, I spent an unforgettable hour slowly "touring" the *Monitor*, close enough to put out a hand and touch that revolutionary iron but for the confines of the submarine. There was the iron belt that surrounded the hull at the waterline, and there, thanks to the disappearance of much of the up-turned, wooden surface hull, I could see portions of the engines, the blowers, the propeller shaft, and more. Most evocative of all, however, was the turret, which has always been the focus of the *Monitor*'s lasting grip on our imaginations. Though upside down and partially covered by the hull, which landed atop it when the vessel capsized in sinking, still much of the turret can be seen, and there still visible in its iron plating were the dents made by the *Virginia*'s shot during their epic duel. Those indentations are perhaps the most eloquent "first-hand" evidence of the Civil War that remain to us today.

Most of all, and despite the dim light and limited visibility, there was the overpowering sense of majesty when this great iron wreck, at once both monument and living document, emerged from the gloom. It seemed to loom over the bare ocean bottom like a small iron mountain. Aboard the submersible all was silence, as four very terrestrial beings of our own time were stunned and speechless as we found ourselves in another world during those minutes in the presence of a great actor from another era.

Perhaps someday more people will be able to make that same ethereal underwater contact with the *Monitor,* or perhaps not. No one yet knows the ultimate fate of all that remains of this magnificent yet fragile artifact from our past. But before long everyone will be able to share at least a part of the view I had, for as readers of *The Monitor Chronicles* will discover, serious efforts are now underway to save as much as possible of the crumbling wreck and bring some of its most significant portions to the surface for lasting preservation and study. Recovery and preservation will take years, but one day everyone may be able to see the engine, portions of the hull, and, most dramatically, the turret itself, almost as I saw them twenty years ago.

Until then, everyone can share the experience of awe and pride and wonder that the men who served aboard her felt through the newly opened letters of one of her seamen, George Geer, who had been in the United States Navy but three weeks when he participated in one of the most famous naval battles of all time. If we cannot be aboard her ourselves, surely the next best thing is to stand beside one who was, peering over his shoulder as he recounts the *Monitor*'s story almost from her birth to her death. If not everyone can yet view the *Monitor* from a submarine port as I did, then Geer's letters afford a wonderful window of their own onto the deck of what he called "this 180 feet of Iron."

THE MONITOR CHRONICLES

... mess which is close ... forth and that
will most keep us in Potatoes and ... this
so we will pass a very ... Winter ...
hope Give my love to Aunt and Uncle ...
to Rachel and the Rest of the family Remember
me to Thomas and Fanny and all ...
Friends I shall look for a ... from you to
morrow and if I do not get it I shall think
... directed to Washington Kiss Hatty and Kitty
me I thought last night when I been
in the Floor if you ware doing the same
... it gets cool I shall while away many
... vening Writting to you It is most Hamm...
... so I will close with much Love
Your Husband
George

devil would co...
not come so we had ...
disapointed yesterday a large ...
Troops were mooved foward towards
Norfolk and this morning about 4 oclo...
a very large Explosion took place an
nothing could be seen of the Merri...
after it so we had orders to mooo...
at once to Norfolk but what we...
... disapointment to learn as we
... Turks had take...

One

THE DUEL

AT THE AGE OF FORTY-THREE, Lieutenant John L. Worden had been twenty-seven years a sailor and seven months a prisoner of the Confederacy when, on January 13, 1862, the Navy Department celebrated his release by placing him in command of its newest and most unusual craft. The ship lay under construction at Green Point, Brooklyn, New York. The deck stretched 172 feet from stem to stern, with a beam of forty-one feet, almost perfectly flat, and covered with iron sheathing. A brass ring twenty feet in diameter sat just forward of the centerline, waiting to accept a cylindrical turret, while the plated box of a pilothouse peeked up near the prow.[1]

This awkward little tub represented the genius of a Swedish immigrant named John Ericsson, who asked that the virtually invulnerable gunboat be called the *Monitor.* With little fanfare, the ironclad hull slid into the water on January 30. To the surprise of many in the

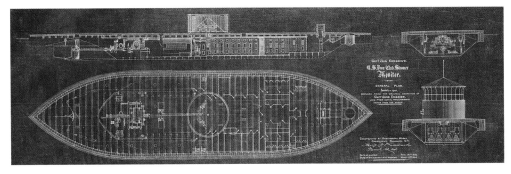

Blueprint of the
U.S. ironclad steamer
Monitor.
FROM THE COLLECTIONS
OF THE MARINERS'
MUSEUM.

shipbuilding trade, it floated, its deck barely eighteen inches above the waterline. Shipfitters and mechanics installed the turret, a nine-foot cylinder with a wall eight inches thick. On one side of the turret, the muzzles of two eleven-inch guns loomed through oblong ports.

A slight man with a long, bushy beard, John Worden's demeanor did not match the classic image of the stern, iron-fisted navy captain. In an age when most naval officers treated their crewmen little better than draft animals, Worden had the knack of winning his men's affection, as well as their respect. Between his affable nature and the renown of his peculiar new ship, he experienced little difficulty shipping a crew. Other skippers were not so lucky. That winter, with so many new vessels under construction and so many men enlisting in the army, commanders at other ports were begging unassigned sailors from other stations to fill their complements. Recruiting agents were

telling potential new hands anything that would persuade them to sign up. Besides his wardroom, steerage, and warrant officers, Worden needed the services of only forty-two souls, and in one visit to the receiving ship *North Carolina* and the frigate *Sabine*, at the Brooklyn Navy Yard, he had more volunteers than he could possibly take.[2]

One of those who stepped forward was a bright, ambitious young man who had just enlisted for a three-year hitch. Twenty-five years old, George Spencer Geer hailed from Troy, New York, where his father and brothers operated a stove foundry. In the forty months since his marriage he had lived in or near New York City, but he had not prospered there. Geer had lost his job and gone into debt to support his wife, Martha, and two young children. The little family lived in an apartment owned by an impatient landlady, Mrs. De Long, at 25 Pitt Street, just off Delancey Street in a crowded tenement neighborhood of what would become famous as the Lower East Side. So, like more than a few men of his station in life, George Geer had joined Abraham Lincoln's navy on February 15, 1862, less to help save the Union than to earn some money and learn a reliable trade. His experience working with the steam engines in his father's foundry may have tipped the scales in his favor, for the navy accepted him as a first-class fireman. It was a rating that paid a tidy thirty dollars a month, whereas a coal heaver or a deck hand earned only eighteen. For Geer, it was a hopeful step into a new life.

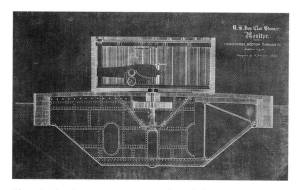

Blueprint showing a transverse section through the Monitor's turret.
From the Collections of The Mariners' Museum.

Geer first shouldered his seabag on board the *North Carolina*, a "devlish old hulk," as he would write of her. The vessel teemed with recruits and with families saying goodbye. Martha appeared, accompanied by her sister Rachel, and she found her husband already beginning his education in the ways of the fledgling United States Navy. He showed her a chunk of the dry, nutritionally bereft hardtack that would make up the better part of his diet over the coming three years. In return, Martha brought her husband a bag of clothing and the few personal items the navy would allow him. Later he would find that she had also tucked three biscuits into his meager cache of belongings—a homely gift of parting from a young wife who would be mostly fending for herself in the months to come.

Amid the hustle that winter day in Brooklyn, Geer handed his wife one month's advance wages—a sum allowed by the paymaster, with the assurance that at the end of each month Martha Geer would receive an additional

Lieutenant John L. Worden,
the Monitor's first commanding officer.
From the Collections of
The Mariners' Museum.

us to know
covered with
get them becaus
here is Boats come
selling them
of us have any
ot buy one if I
nough to eat
ways palatable
makes up for
t to Washington
to Norfolk and
rimack but
vy told him
we all know
nts to distinguish
as Capt Worden
id Worden will
as a chance
ing for him to
ove to Rach and
and all enquiring
d if he could
ay mornings we
Your Husband

U S Steamer Monitor
March 26 1862

Dear Martha

I received your kin[d]
no Paper I may
and I may not
to hear you ar[e]
becaus you w[ere]
money for some
you are very on[e]
I know I was
trouble about it th[e]
having a crying
sp[ell] I had supposed th[at]
you would be able to get it at t[he]
end of this month but keep up you[r]
courage we have always lived and
had enough so far to keep us f[rom]
actual want but dear Wife we m[ust]
hope for the best times will chan[ge]
with us some time and we will

George S. Geer, in uniform, in a contemporary newspaper photograph. FROM THE COLLECTIONS OF THE MARINERS' MUSEUM.

allotment of half her husband's pay. As she would soon discover, however, the U.S. Navy in 1862 was itself struggling to make ends meet while supporting the war effort, and navy agents eager to snare recruits might promise almost anything. George Geer had been told that the advanced funds would be taken from his pay only gradually, and that the monthly allotments could begin immediately.[3] In truth, Martha Geer would have to scrape by for months before seeing another nickel.[4]

Another lesson George Geer would soon learn was that in some ways life aboard the *Monitor* was like that of no other navy ship. On a standard vessel, the various military strata each found their quarters in a traditional location, with status usually increasing toward the stern: the captain's cabin and stateroom were always located aft, with the other commissioned officers' staterooms just forward, on either side of the wardroom. Steerage officers, including the relatively new naval class of engineers, would be quartered ahead of the wardroom, and the warrant officers—boatswain, gunner, master at arms, and quartermasters—might have their own segregated location as well, if the ship were large enough. Forwardmost on the old ships lay the berth deck, beneath the

forecastle, where the common sailors, petty officers, and on steamers the firemen would sling their hammocks.

On the *Monitor*, this social architecture was reversed. Lieutenant Worden's rooms were tucked far forward, in the bow of the ship ahead of the wardroom, where he and the ironclad's nine other commissioned officers took their meals. Directly aft of Worden's stateroom and cabin, on either side of the wardroom, slept the executive officer, Lieutenant Samuel Dana Greene, and the ship's acting assistant paymaster, William Frederick Keeler. The surgeon's cabin lay aft of Keeler's, on the other side of a blind door. Most of the rest of the commissioned officers crowded into six little staterooms to port and starboard. Assistant engineers, steerage officers, and warrant officers were out of luck: the little *Monitor* offered no other housing save the berth deck, which stretched aft of the staterooms to a point beneath the turret. This open space, measuring about sixteen by twenty-five feet, was home to forty-nine men. In theory, the setup was livable because two watches alternated duty and only about two dozen crew would sleep there at any given moment. Behind the berth deck, the *Monitor* was all boilers and engines.[5]

 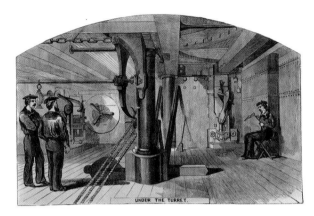

THE BERTH DECK.

UNDER THE TURRET.

Details of an engraving depicting the Monitor's *wardroom, berth deck, and the captain's cabin.*

FROM THE COLLECTIONS OF THE MARINERS' MUSEUM.

Gideon Welles, Mr. Lincoln's secretary of the navy, itched to see the *Monitor* at Hampton Roads, Virginia—an itch fed by reports that at the Norfolk Navy Yard Confederate shipbuilders were nearing completion of their own ironclad. Using the hull and engines of the former United States frigate *Merrimack,* they had built a floating battery of ten guns, protected by sloping walls of oak and iron. On February 20, Welles decided to scratch his itch. He ordered Worden to submit a list of the *Monitor*'s crew and head for Hampton Roads, adding that Worden could expect at least one other ship to accompany her to Virginia. After six days of preparations, on the evening of February 26, 1862, the last of the ammunition went into the *Monitor*'s shot lockers and magazine.

The next morning, under the pelting snow and wind of a northeaster, the strange little craft steamed out of the navy yard into the East River. Almost immediately, the helmsman found the *Monitor*'s wheel stiff—in fact, so unworkable that he couldn't get adequate leverage on the rudder. Like a waterborne Ping-Pong ball, the *Monitor* began to careen madly from one side of the river to the other. Worden ordered her back to the dock, taking a towline from one of his escort vessels to avoid smashing about in the crowded navy yard.

For two days John Ericsson puzzled over this problem. The quartermaster, who had struggled with the helm, suggested that perhaps a bigger wheel would allow better purchase on the cables that turned the rudder. Instead, Ericsson enhanced the leverage of the cables by extending the reach of the tiller head arms, a solution that turned out to work reasonably well. On March 1 Worden advised Welles that Ericsson expected to finish his modifications the next day, and planned a test run for March 3. But when the moment came, the March sky opened up with a deluge so fierce Worden returned the *Monitor* to the navy yard yet again. Only three days later, when the skies lightened, would the "cheesebox on a raft" go to sea at last.[6]

Portrait photograph of John Ericsson, reportedly taken in 1863. This photograph is included in an album compiled by John Worden and is now in the collections of The Mariners' Museum.

Meanwhile, Fireman George Geer had been working so diligently preparing the ship's engines, coaling the bunkers, and storing ammunition and supplies that he had been unable to write his wife a farewell letter. Now, out in the river, the little ship lay barely a mile from his home on Pitt Street. Gazing shoreward, he knew he would have no chance to cover that mile before they left for wherever they were bound. If he did not know his destination, he at least knew that it

When I go on deck to day and look over towards home it makes the tears start to think I am so near you and cannot be with you. Oh, how I would like to see all of you.

— MARCH 2, 1862

would take the *Monitor* out where heavy seas could surge across its flat deck and threaten every aperture, and even a landlubber like himself might have deduced that this was the most dangerous thing the iron-clad could do. While mechanics grappled with the steering apparatus, Geer seated himself before an overturned bucket and began the first of scores of letters that Martha Geer would receive and carefully preserve during the course of the war.

U.S.S. Monitor
February [March] 2, 1862

Dear Wife

At last I have a fiew moments to write to you but I have so much to say and so many questions to ask I hardly know where to commence. I will commence by telling you what I am writing on. I have for my desk a water pail turned up side down so you see we have not all the improvements of the age. I do not think I have gained any in flesh, but our living is holeson [*wholesome*] and will keep me from getting the gout. Matty when I come home I will be able to apreciate your cooking if I neaver did before.

    I suppose you saw by the Papers that we started and had to come back. The Ship would not stear. She went first into the Ships on the N.Y. side and then over slam in to the Brooklyn dock, but all the trouble was our stearing wheel was to small. We will have a larger one done to day and shall go to sea again in the morning.

When I go on deck to day and look over towards home it makes the tears start to think I am so near you and cannot be with you. Oh, how I would like to see all of you.

Our ship is so much more comfortable than the old North Carolina but we are not in order yet and have to work most of the time. As soon as we are in shape I will have only eight hours of work out of twenty-four, so you see I will not have to work hard. The pay master or Purser says he will make out that alotment and send it from Fortress Monroe so it will be in New York before the money is due me.

I tride very hard to get on shore to day but could not. I think if I did not owe the Government anything I mint [*might*] get ashore but until I am out of their debt I may as well give up getting off.

. . . It is so cold we most freese nights and I am most frose writing this Lettor. I will be glad when we get where it is warmer. Tell me in your Lettor if Rachel is with you much and give my love to her. Also to Wm. Henry, Kate, and Jonny [*members of Geer's extended family*]. Kiss both the Babys about 24 times apiec for me and dont let them get sick and as for you I have got no love for you, you have it all. Now I am to cold to write more. This from your

Affectionate husband,
Geo. S. Geer

In Virginia, military officials were receiving ominous reports that the *Merrimack*—rechristened the CSS *Virginia*—was complete and ready to attack Newport News. Secretary Welles decided that the *Monitor* should turn northwest once she reached the Chesapeake Bay, and come up to Washington. This detour would give politicians and others a closer look at the ironclad—and, possibly, she would be available to help protect the capital if the need arose. On March 6, Welles telegraphed the commandant of the Brooklyn Navy Yard with instructions for Worden, but his telegram did not reach New York until that evening. By then the *Monitor* was gone.[7]

Lieutenant Worden dismissed the harbor pilot after the little *Monitor* passed the bar, at 4:00 P.M. that Thursday. The sun still shone brightly. The *Monitor* could not seem to reach its promised headway of eight knots, though, and in order to make the best speed under fair skies Worden took a line from the tugboat *Seth Low*. As Welles had promised, two little screw steamers, the *Currituck* and the *Sachem*, ran alongside. Each of them mounted only four thirty-two-pounder carronades and a single twenty-pounder rifle. The ironclad they escorted might have sent either of them to the bottom with a single shot. The unavoidable inference was that they were intended to serve not as protection, but as rescue vessels. More than a few people believed that the improbable *Monitor* would never be a dependable craft at sea.

The first test of her seaworthiness arrived with the following dawn. As the wind picked up, the seas began to stir. Low waves washed over the deck, filtering into openings and leaking under the turret. Water gushed onto the lower deck, soaking every compartment before the pumps expelled it. Water poured down the temporary blower pipes, the mouths of which opened only six feet off the deck; the drive belts that turned these ventilators dragged once they were soaked, and at last they snapped, shutting off the outside air. As men dropped from the fumes, Chief Engineer Alban Stimers and First Assistant Engineer Isaac Newton led the rest of their department into the engine compartment and set to work. One by one the firemen too became dizzy or fainted. They staggered or were dragged to fresh air at the top of the turret. Stimers struggled on, persuading the blowers to run haphazardly, though the air was still stale and the boiler fires didn't have enough draft. Without efficient boilers, the pressure for the auxiliary pump engines dropped. Toward midnight, water started gaining on the pumps, and as the seas rose the blower pipes were in danger again. It must have been easy, in that moment, to foresee an early end to the *Monitor*, but as the morning arrived the wind began to subside. Every man aboard was drenched, none had slept for fifty-three hours, but the *Monitor* was still there.[8]

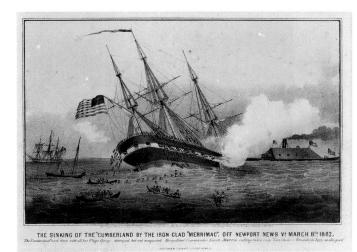

THE SINKING OF THE "CUMBERLAND" BY THE IRON CLAD "MERRIMAC", OFF NEWPORT NEWS Vᵃ MARCH 8ᵗʰ 1862.

Lithograph showing the CSS Virginia *sinking the* Cumberland *and bearing the inscription: "Sketched by N. Newman, Newport News, Virginia. The* Cumberland *went down with all her flags flying destroyed, but not conquered. Her gallant Commander Lieut. Morris, calling to his crew, 'Give them a broadside, boys, as she goes.'"*
FROM THE COLLECTIONS OF THE MARINERS' MUSEUM.

While the men on the *Monitor* struggled to keep her afloat, the crew of the *Virginia* were preparing for a fight with the Union fleet in Hampton Roads. Captain Franklin Buchanan, commander of the Confederacy's squadron on the James River, boarded the *Virginia* himself at the old Gosport Navy Yard. Late on the morning of March 8, as the *Monitor* made her way down the coast off Cape Charles, Buchanan started up the Elizabeth River past Norfolk. Two one-gun steamers, the *Beaufort* and *Raleigh*, accompanied him. They passed friendly batteries at Craney Island and Sewell's Point, where the *Virginia* veered toward Newport News Point.

An assortment of United States ships lay between Newport News and Old Point Comfort, where Fort Monroe stood vigilant. Collectively they carried 291 guns to the *Virginia*'s ten, but Buchanan maneuvered the *Virginia* as if she were impervious. For all intents and purposes, she was. When the fifty-gun frigate *Congress* opened fire with a broadside, clearing smoke revealed the *Virginia* unscathed. She responded with a four-gun volley that blasted through the *Congress*'s timbers like they were matchsticks. Using her ram and guns, the *Virginia* next sank the Union sloop of war *Cumberland,* sending to their deaths a hundred luckless men.

And so the battle went. Returning to the wounded *Congress,* which her skipper had run aground in an attempt to avoid total destruction, Buchanan used the armament of his iron-sheathed ship to pound her into submission.

Other big Federal ships that came to help, mostly under the motive power of tugs, fared little better. The *Minnesota* grounded in the tidally shallow north channel of the James River. Likewise striking low water, the *St. Lawrence* grounded short of the *Minnesota,* and the *Roanoke* couldn't even reach that far. Only the dropping tide prevented the *Virginia* from coming up to finish the *Minnesota,* and her gunners threw shells at the hapless Union frigate for over an hour, from a distance of over a mile. It had been a fair day's work, and the Confederates expected to come back in the morning to finish up.[9]

All that could save the Union fleet, it seemed, was the *Monitor,* which at that moment lay off Cape Henry, twenty miles away. Hearing the echo of gunfire, Worden deduced that the *Virginia* had made her appearance. He set the crew to trimming the *Monitor* for battle, disassembling the temporary blower pipes and removing the almost useless caulking under the turret. The men labored as well as they could, but no one had slept for two and a half days and most of the crew—except George Geer and some others—were seasick. By the time the ship was ready to fight and had covered the last ten miles to Fort Monroe, it was 9:00 P.M. Hampton Roads at last lay quiet, but six miles to the west the burning hulk of the *Congress* illuminated the night sky.

If Federal officers had imagined the *Monitor* as their salvation, many of them winced when they saw what it actually looked like. The black hull was barely more than half the length of the Confederate leviathan, and it sat so low that only the squat turret seemed to rise above the water. *Monitor* carried one sixth as many men as the *Virginia* and only two guns to the ten of her opponent. In an era when the number of guns implied the strength of a vessel, the *Monitor*'s brace of Dahlgrens hardly inspired confidence. (No one on that side of the bay yet knew that two of the *Virginia*'s guns had been disabled by the dying *Cumberland*.) Though the other grounded Union ships had broken free, the hapless *Minnesota* remained stuck. Worden dropped anchor not far away around 1:00 A.M., in time for the crew to witness the death of the *Congress* in a spectacular explosion.

"A volcano seemed to open instantaneously," recalled Paymaster Keeler in a letter to his wife. "Pieces of burning timbers, exploding shells, huge fragments of the wreck, grenades & rockets filled the air & fell sparkling & hissing in all directions." Although the *Monitor* lay a couple of miles distant from the *Congress*, Keeler noted that the blast even seemed to lift the ironclad out of the water.

Worden couldn't be certain of the *Virginia*'s draft, about twice his own, and once again he kept both watches awake all night as they lay waiting for the rising tide. When the sun came up on March 9, George Geer had not closed his eyes in seventy-two hours.[10]

Geer had taken his morning watch in the engine room when, about 8:00 A.M., a lookout sighted the *Virginia* moving away from Sewell's Point. As expected, she turned for the *Minnesota*. Worden called up the anchor and sent the crew to quarters— posts that sailors of a later day would call battle stations.

Aboard *Virginia*, Lieutenant Catesby Jones had taken over from Captain Buchanan, who had been wounded in the previous day's battle. Concentrating on the marooned *Minnesota*, Jones ignored the *Monitor* until its black pillbox turret revolved and sent an eleven-inch solid shot his way. Realizing that the bizarre little object was an enemy vessel, Jones turned his guns on her. The world's first fight between ironclad warships was under way.

Fireman Geer was sweating out his watch in the engine room when the battle began, shifting later to the shot room, where

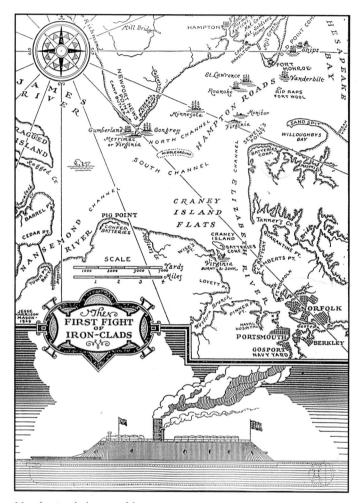

Map showing the location of the engagement between the USS Monitor *and CSS* Virginia.

his job was to help keep the gunners in the turret supplied with ammunition. As the guns reverberated, he pondered the fate of his family—Martha, whom he often called Mattie, and his two sons, one still a babe in arms—if he were to go down with the ship.

"I often thought of you and the little darlings when the fight was going on and what should become of you should I be killed," he would write later. Events would enable him to add the cocky coda: "...but I should have no more such fears as our ship resisted everything they could fire at her as though they were spit balls."

As the battle unfolded, the gunners were learning their trade as they practiced it, for they had never previously loaded or fired the guns they now worked. After each round, the turret had to be revolved away for reloading. The heavy port covers were difficult to close and open, and closing them shut out all light, but with only one real opponent it was safe enough just to spin the ports away from the *Virginia*'s fire. The control wheel for the pony engines that operated the turret, soaked during the trip down, had rusted, and Acting Master Louis N. Stodder lacked the strength to turn it. Chief Engineer Stimers, however, had spent most of his adult life turning wrenches, and he now managed to break the rust free. Stimers, who had come along as a nominal inspector of the new ship, had once served as an engineer on the very *Merrimack* from which the *Virginia* had been reconstructed. He was proving an invaluable passenger, but after a time even he found it difficult to stop the turret in time for an aimed shot.

Improvising, Lieutenant Greene, who commanded in the turret, decided to fire as the guns swept by their target. Jostling in the cramped space, eight men worked each piece. Worden and a volunteer pilot from another ship occupied the pilothouse, with the quartermaster at the helm. A speaking tube connected the two locations, but when the turret was set free a runner had to carry orders and information down from the turret, through the berth deck and wardroom, and up to the pilothouse. As the *Monitor* and *Virginia* vied for victory, Paymaster Keeler was the usual go-between.

The first shot to hit the turret made a depression several inches deep. Stimers quickly gauged, then assuaged fears: denting, he asserted, was the most the enemy could do to them. The gun crews went to

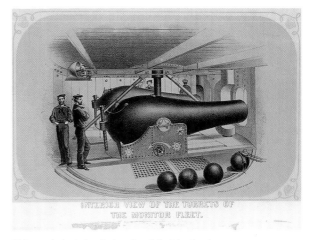

Lithograph depicting the interior of the Monitor's *turret.*
<small>From the Collections of
The Mariners' Museum.</small>

The Monitor's *original chief engineer,
Alban Stimers.*
<small>From the Collections of
The Mariners' Museum.</small>

<small>The Duel</small>

work with a will, stripping off their shirts in the growing heat of combat.[11]

For an hour and a half it was all sweat and sulfur in the turret. Gunpowder residue coated the bare-chested gunners to their waists. In the whirling casemate, no one

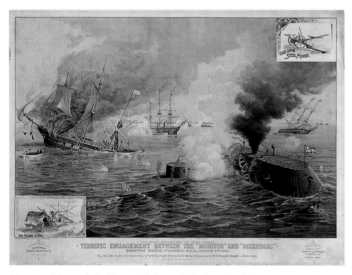

This 1862 lithograph by Henry Bill depicts "The First Battle Between 'Iron' Ships of War." It bears the inscription "The MONITOR, 2 guns, and the MERRIMAC, 10 guns. The MERRIMAC was crippled and the Rebel Fleet driven off."
FROM THE COLLECTIONS OF THE MARINERS' MUSEUM.

could see the results of their toil; the job grew dangerously monotonous. At 10:00 A.M. a shot struck the turret near its engine lever. Leaning against the wall where the blow

struck, Stimers, Stodder, and a seaman were knocked to the floor. Stimers quickly recovered his feet, but the other two men had to be carried below, where the surgeon administered a few shots of the sailor's cure-all.

The Virginia tried to ram, despite the fact most of her ram had gone down with the Cumberland. That deficiency, the Monitor's armor, and Worden's quick thinking prevented real damage. Seeing the attack coming, Worden gave Keeler a message for the turret commander: when the two ships collided, Greene was to let fly with both barrels. Then, just before the Virginia hit, Worden directed his helmsman to veer off, to reduce the force of the blow. At the instant of impact, Greene fired and struck the enemy's forward casemate with a solid shot.

Greene himself fired every gun, lest a careless hand blow the Monitor's own pilot-house off the deck. Heads were pounding inside the turret from the roar of the guns, but after several hours the turret shot racks lay empty. The turret had to stop turning while the powder division carried up fresh ammunition through a pair of scuttle holes in the turret floor and the deck, so Worden ordered the ship out of action. Now George Geer and his mates went to work, hoisting the ponderous balls up to the gunners. It was easy enough to hand up bags of gunpowder, but the projectiles were another matter. Knowing that each shot weighed 180 pounds, Worden ordered Mr. Keeler to open the spirit locker and dole out a bit of stimulation for everyone.[12]

So long did the *Monitor's* operators linger that the Confederates imagined they had put their peculiar opponent out of action. But the *Monitor* turned back for more, and soon the two lay only yards apart again, exchanging volleys that would have destroyed any other vessel afloat, anywhere in the world. Seven shots rang off the *Monitor's* turret to no visible effect, and several ricocheted off the deck or the slim slice of freeboard. The only vulnerable spot on John Ericsson's little invention was the pilot-house, sitting so small and so far forward. It had been built to take abuse, framed of iron beams a foot thick. One shot bounded harmlessly off, but as Worden brought the ship in close, the *Virginia* aimed a shell at the pilothouse. It exploded in front of the viewing slot in the same moment as Worden peered out, smashing one of the iron beams and prying the slot open. Blinded, Worden fell back and ordered the quartermaster to sheer off.

The viewing slot in the Monitor's *turret, as represented in a contemporary engraving.*
FROM THE COLLECTIONS OF THE MARINERS' MUSEUM.

Keeler helped Worden to the foot of the ladder and sent for the executive officer. Greene rushed forward from the turret, leaving Stimers to command the guns. Then, before taking command of his first ship, Greene guided Worden to the couch in the captain's cabin, where Surgeon Daniel C. Logue began plucking slivers of iron and paint from the swollen, blackened eyes.

As Greene took his place in the battered pilothouse, he scanned the water. The *Virginia* had started toward the Elizabeth River, and Greene assumed it had taken flight. In fact, Lieutenant Jones had made the same assumption about his Union adversary as he watched her sheer away when Worden was wounded. He counted this as the second time he had silenced the smaller ship's guns, and headed

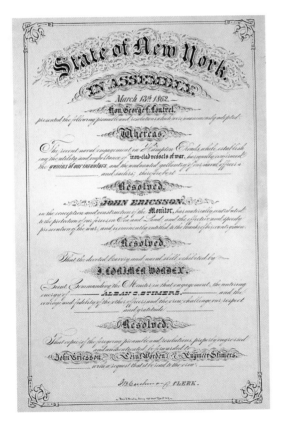

back to Norfolk with the other Confederate ships following in his wake. Greene, having satisfied the *Monitor*'s original instructions to protect the *Minnesota*, dropped anchor. It was just past noon, and the crew ran up on deck for a long-awaited glimpse of the sun and some fresh air. None of them had been outside for a solid twelve hours, and the engineer department—including George Geer —had been locked up below, sweltering in the boiler room and in the storage compartments, since the previous afternoon.[13]

Stimers, the visiting engineer and inspector, recorded his observations in a notebook. He counted seven big dents in the turret, none of which cracked any of the eight layers of one-inch iron. Yet the solid iron beam that protected the pilothouse, measuring a foot by nine inches, was broken nearly in two by the sixty-eight-pound rifle shell that had wounded Lieutenant Worden. In all, Stimers tallied twenty-one dents from Confederate fire, with no real damage except to the pilothouse.

From the deck of the *Minnesota*, Assistant Secretary of the Navy Gustavus Fox had watched the battle. Now he ordered a boat to take him to the *Monitor*, where he would graciously thank the men for their efforts.

"Considering that the officers, crew, and

engineers had a horrible passage," Fox would later write a U.S. senator, "arrived at 10 P.M., and handled an untried experiment without previous drill, and went into action at 8 A.M. the next day, their conduct is beyond praise."

One of those officers left the *Monitor* that afternoon, never to return. At the request of the assistant secretary, Lieutenant Worden was carried up from his cabin and placed on a tug. His crewmen, who had known him less than a month, stood by to cheer him madly as he passed them. From the tugboat, Worden boarded a steamer for Washington, where, slowly, his eyesight would return. Then, hours after their breakfast had been interrupted by the call to stand to quarters, the *Monitor* crew sat down to dinner.

Honors and souvenirs of the battle between the Monitor *and the* Virginia. OPPOSITE PAGE *Testimonial to John Ericsson, Lieutenant John L. Worden, and Alban Stimers, from the New York State legislature. March 13, 1862. National Oceanographic and Atmospheric Administration;* ABOVE *Enameled souvenir spoon commemorating the battle of the* Monitor *and the* Virginia; BELOW *Souvenir scrimshaw showing Lieutenant Worden and CSS* Virginia *Captain Franklin Buchanan.* FROM THE COLLECTIONS OF THE MARINERS' MUSEUM.

Though pushed to the limits of human endurance, the men still had to finish their day's work. As they toiled, they enjoyed the illusion that they had driven the *Virginia* away. Yet they were too exhausted to understand the historic implications of their clash in shallow water. Their duel that Sunday had foretold the end of the wooden warships that surrounded them. Meanwhile, the *Monitor* sailors neither noticed nor cared that they had helped to open a new naval era.

U S Monitor Fortress Monroe
March 10 1862

Dr Wife

I improve the first
moment I have had sence we
left New York to write you and
I assure you I am doing under
great dificulty as I have not
slep over foor hours in three
days but as soon as I finnish
it I shall turn in and sleep
untill 8 oclock it is now three
then I will be at the fires untill
12 and then can sleep untill 6
unless the Merrymac should
make her apperance again. I
I shall write you very little
about our Fight as you will
see it all in the Papers I was
on duty in the fire room when
the action commenced but was

Letter from George Geer to his wife, Martha, March 10, 1862.
FROM THE COLLECTIONS OF THE MARINERS' MUSEUM.

Soon naval and army officers crawled all over the ship in dark blue and bright braid, marveling at its machinery and commending the crew. As he wrote to his wife, his eyes drooping with fatigue, Geer cheated future historians by advising her to seek details of the battle from the newspapers.

U.S. Monitor, Fortress Monroe
March 10, 1862

Dr Wife

. . . I shall write you very little about our Fight as you will see it all in the Papers. I was on duty in the fire room when the action commenced but was relieved and went to my station hoisting up shot and shell to the Tower Guns. . . . Our Ship is crowded with Generals and Officers of all grades both army and Navy. They are wild with joy and say if any of us come to the Fort we can have all we want free, as we have saved 100s of lives and millions of property to the Government.

. . . I have enough to tell you to make twenty Lettors but cannot think of anything. I am clear of my Coald and feel well with the exception of want of sleep. I must close at once as there is a man for the lettors.

Your Husband
George

George Geer had more than half his life remaining, but he had already taken part in the most momentous event he would ever see. For the rest of his days, he would be known as one of the few who had been inside the *Monitor* during its brief and early moment of glory.

THE DUEL

Dear Wife

hand all right and Your Letter and the Silk
Ikeant I kept for my self and the colored silk
could have Sold the colored silk but would n
Iwant untill I see how much I want of it m
self I get for what silk I sold $3.50 so you
think it very well off of it besides having what
Iwant as one of the Coal Heavers
last evening and I dont think
granted if we go to Washington
have got them prety well supp
I look Kinver and Serens
the lock as now as I took

Two

THE STANDOFF

THE NEXT TWO MONTHS crept by for the *Monitor* and her crew. After the intense excitement attending their arrival, the ironclad was forced to sit idle, waiting for the *Virginia* to emerge on another foray. During the lull, George Geer grew homesick, even as the *Monitor* crew reveled in their success. His letter of March 15 perfectly captured this incongruous mix of emotions:

"Your kind and much looked for lettor came to hand, and at a time when I was very down hearted, and it revived me at once. I see you are highly elated at the success of the Monitor but hold on, we have only commenced. You will soon hear more from us. We expect every day to see the Merimack poking herself down here and she will not get away from us again. We will capture her or Sink her the next time."

Unlike most soldiers and many sailors, Geer could depend on regular mail to buoy his spirits. He and Martha had made a pact: they would

The Monitor *paymaster, William F. Keeler.*
From the Collections of The Mariners' Museum.

correspond without fail each Sunday and Wednesday so that each could calculate when a letter might be due. Paymaster Keeler received almost as frequent mail from his wife in Illinois, but by the time he opened them their contents had aged as much as a fortnight.[1] Martha Geer's letters usually reached her husband on the second day after she mailed them because mail steamers plied daily between New York and Fort Monroe. They thus became valuable sources of timely information for Geer (and his shipmates). Other times the exchanges were simply the dealings of two people trying to share their cares and affection from a distance. When Martha sent him the ingredients for making a simple confection to enliven the dull navy food, Geer wrote back that the experiment had failed for the want of a mixing pot. By the time Geer wrote to Martha in mid-March, however, there was much more distressing news: Paymaster Keeler had informed Geer that his wife would not be able to draw money from his pay until the first of May, rather than the first of April. Her plight had grown so desperate that she had pawned her wedding ring, as the March 15 letter indicates Geer surmised; now, for an entire month, she would have to survive by borrowing.

> We expect every day to see the Merimack poking herself down here and she will not get away from us again. We will capture her or sink her the next time.
>
> — MARCH 15, 1862

U.S.S. Monitor
Hampton Roads
March 15, 1862

Dr Mattie

. . . I have written to day a four paged lettor to Mother and I think you will not be troubled for money in future although I said but very little about it. You may have money, I know where you got it and I know how many kindnesses and obligations we are under to Sistor Rachel, and hope we may live to be able to repay them with Interest.

I am very sorry to hear that Willie [*their older son, William Clarke Geer, who was not yet three*] has been sick but you say he is better. Uncle, I suppose has one of his old attacks. Have you got a letter from Aunt, and what does she say about my going?

. . . The Assistant Secretary of the Navy was here and said we should be all well rewarded for our galiant conduct but did not state how, but I suppose with a meddle.

. . . I would not be surprised if I were to date my Lettors from Norfolk in less than two weeks. We live much bettor here than we did on that devlish old hulk North Carolina.

. . . Kiss the Babys for me and tell them Papa will come home soon to see them.

Your affectionate,
George

Meanwhile, the *Monitor* had assumed a key role in the Union strategy in Virginia. Major General George McClellan, the young commander of the Army of the Potomac, wanted to land his divisions at Fort Monroe and march them up the peninsula between the York and James rivers to Richmond. He would take his supplies from successive riverside landings

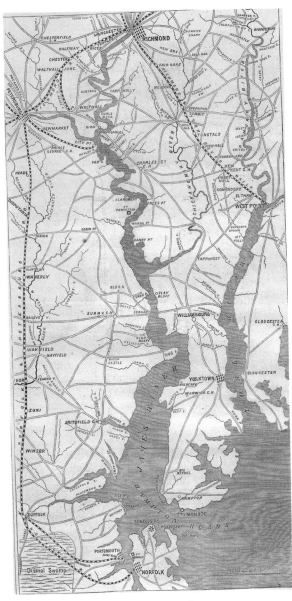

Map showing "The Seat of War in Virginia,"
Harper's Weekly, May 24, 1862.
FROM THE COLLECTIONS OF THE MARINERS' MUSEUM.

protected by the navy's powerful gunboats, which sported ordnance that outweighed anything the Confederates could field outside siege lines. A craft as seemingly invulnerable as the *Virginia* could stymie McClellan's plan, so on March 12, he asked Gustavus Fox if the *Monitor* could neutralize the "*Merrimack*" sufficiently to allow the army to use Fort Monroe as a base of operations. The *Monitor* had been strengthened a bit since her fight with the *Virginia*, for Chief Engineer Stimers had reinforced the vulnerable pilothouse with thick, sloping walls. Cautiously optimistic, Fox replied that John Ericsson's little ironclad might even be able to sink her Confederate counterpart.

McClellan also asked about blocking the mouth of the Elizabeth River with sunken hulks, a plan that would expose the *Monitor* to enemy fire during the reduction of the Confederate batteries on Sewell's Point. Unwilling to risk the Union's only hope against the *Virginia*, the navy declined. So, encouraged by Fox's assessment, McClellan decided to proceed. Thus it was that on March 17, because George Geer and fifty-seven of his shipmates lay at Hampton Roads on their peculiar vessel, the first of more than 120,000 Union soldiers boarded steamships at Alexandria, Virginia, for Fort Monroe.[2]

Dr Wife

. . . You asked me if I recvd that Gumarabic and candy. Yes, but I had no way of
dissolving it and I had to eat it and let it dissolve in my mouth. It tasted <u>very bad,</u>
especialy the candy. I think you asked me some other questions but as I have no place
to keep your lettors I burn them as soon as I read them and if you ask me anything
I do not answer you may know I have forgotten it.

I have been in great trouble since Sunday. The Purcer called us all in the Cabin and had
us sign our half pay tickets. He told me the first payment would be made on mine the last
day of April. That devilish scoundrel that shiped us told me that our advance would be
taken out gradually and that the alotment would be paid the end of the first month but in
place of that I have to work out the advance and have one months pay due me before we
can get any money on my account. If I had have known that when I shiped I would not
have shiped, but here I am now and must make the best of it, but after you get the first
payment my heart will be at ease. Untill then I shall have constant worryment.

. . . We are having very easy and very lazy times laying here waiting for the Merimack.
I have been in the Navy one month to day and I have worked so hard the time has sliped
by very quick but know [*now*] we are doing nothing and it commences to drag very slow.

. . . It was a very agreeable change to come from the cold winds of New York to this balmy
and warm climate. It is as warm here now as it will be in New York the first of May. . . .

. . . I done the Cook a favor and on Sunday morning he gave me half of a Mackrel and
two buscuit. I thought when I was eating them that perhaps you was eating the same but
then I had no Willey to give some to, no Wife to pore out a good cup of coffee, no Sunday
Paper to read, no little Gilley [*their second son, Gilbert*] to talk to. Oh when I get home
again I will know how to apreciate a loving Wife's society, although I cannot love you any
bettor than I always have. . . .

Your Husband
Geo. S. Geer

Military personnel were cautioned to keep quiet about the massive troop movement, but this early form of military censorship was largely voluntary. The letter George Geer penned on March 24, 1862, speaks plainly:

"An order has come to us this morning that we would not be alowed to send any more Lettors after to day for 10 days," he informed Martha, "so if you do not receive any Lettors from me you will know the reason, but you must not neglect to write me as Lettors can come to us the same. The reason of the order is that they are bringing a large boddy of Troops here for the purpos of taking Yorktown and they are afraid it mint [might] get in the Papers. It was a splendid sight yesterday to see fourteen Steamboats loaded down with troops come in. They all had to steam up and take a look at the Cheese Box, as they call us, and it was chear on chear. There is some 60 or 70 Thousand troops here and moore to arive. Don't you go and give that information to any Secesh."

This same letter also voices the stirring of George Geer's thoughts about the possibilities his *Monitor* service could open up:

"Gilbert [his younger brother, Gilbert Geer, Jr.] gives me some very good advise: he says that as soon as I think I am capable he will try and get me apointed as an Engineer through a Mr. Filley of Troy who is intimate with the Secretary of the Navy. I am watching every thing very clost and learning all I can."

> *It was a splendid sight yesterday to see fourteen Steamboats loaded down with troops come in. They all had to steam up and take a look at the Cheese Box, as they call us, and it was chear on chear.*
>
> — MARCH 24, 1862

Lieutenant Commander William N. Jeffers,
who took command of the Monitor
shortly after its encounter with the Virginia.
FROM THE COLLECTIONS OF THE MARINERS' MUSEUM.

The *Monitor* now had a new commander, one considerably less popular than Worden. For several days Lieutenant Thomas O. Selfridge, a
survivor of the *Cumberland*'s crew, had occupied the captain's cabin, but
on March 12 the more experienced Lieutenant William N. Jeffers arrived
to supersede him. Jeffers was a chunky, impersonable fellow with a bad
temper, and Paymaster Keeler quickly concluded that Jeffers did not
own Lieutenant Worden's "noble kindness of heart & quiet unassuming
manner."

"Our new Capt. is a rigid disciplinarian," Keeler informed his wife,
"of quick imperious temper & domineering disposition. . . . I keep my
seat next to him at the table but do not find it as pleasant as when
Capt. Worden filled his place."

Fireman Geer's assessment of the new skipper would eventually
make Keeler's look charitable.[3] Yet Geer bided his time, watching
troop movements and taking care to live as frugally as possible so that
he might provide more money for Martha and the boys.

Dear Martha

. . . I am very glad to hear that you are not down hearted becaus you will not get any money for some time. I suppose you are very much disapointed, and I know I was in so much trouble about it that I could not help having a crying spell over it, as I had supposed that you would be able to get it at the end of this month. . . .

. . . I believe I have not told you before how much my <u>Grog</u> is. By not drinking it I get $1.25 per month, which will most cloath me.

. . . I am writting this while on watch by permission of the Engineer [at] two oclock in the morning, and am thinking of you fast a sleep with Rach and the two darlings. We are having a very fine sight, looking at the Transports come in with Troops and stores . . . There is to be here in all I hear one hundred and fifteen Thousand Troops.

It is very provoking for us to know that the bottom here is covered with Oysters and we cannot get them becaus we have no dredge. There is boats come along side some times selling them, 12 cts. [per] Doz., but very fiew of us have any money and I would not buy one if I had money. We get enough to eat, although it is not always palatable, but a good apatite makes up for that. . . .

Our Captain sent to Washington for permission to go up to Norfolk and take or sink the Merimack, but the Secretary of the Navy told him to stay where he was. We all know what he wants: he wants to distinguish himself with her as Captain Worden don, and he is afraid Worden will be back before he has a chance—and we are all praying for him to come soon.

Your Husband
George

Geer had not served long in Mr. Lincoln's navy when he met first-hand the root cause of the war that had engulfed him. A contraband, or runaway slave, had made his way to the deck of the *Monitor*, bringing with him the usual mix of information and misinformation about the enemy. This man claimed to have seen thirty Confederate dead after the ironclads' clash, though in truth no one had been killed on either vessel.

U.S. Steamer Monitor
Fortress Monroe, March 30, 1862

Dr Martha

. . . We had a Counterband on board yesterday that ran away from Norfolk. . . . He says he saw the Merimack on Monday and that she was then in dock repairing. He says he was in the Hospital and helped to lay out fifteen boddys and that there was fiftenn more killed besides a large number wounded, and they say all the damage was done by us. I don't think we will get another chance at her unless we go up there.

Boredom was becoming firmly entrenched on the *Monitor*, leaving Geer with little to recount of his daily life except the minutiae of a be-calmed sailor's lot. Hence he recorded for Martha details of shipboard existence which, more than a century later, provide unique glimpses of that bygone moment.

U.S. Steamer Monitor
Hampton Roads, April 2, 1862

Your Lettor came to hand to day. It was rather small, but half a loaf is bettor than none. . . . You must not expect much news from me as there is very little transpiring on this 180 feet of Iron. . . .

I expected to draw a pair of Shoes yesterday, but they had none to fit me but fine ones, so I got none. I do not intend to draw any cloathing if I can help, but after you commence to get money I shall have you send me what I want. I want Over halls and Shirts very bad, but these Pants and Shirts have got so Greesy and dirty that Overhalls would do them no good. I have one pair of pants that I have not had on yet, and I am trying to keep them for a mustering Suit.

How much did you pay for that Soap? I wish you had not bought it, as we can get all the fresh Water we want, and that Soap is so much Alkali that it takes the Skin off my hands. When I tell you to send me a box I will give you a list of things I want. We can get no Soap on board but Salt Water Soap, and it is very soft and not as good as that you bought. They charge 22¢ pr lb.

I hope and pray you get mooved without braking every thing to pieces. See if you cannot make a bargain with the carman to pay for any thing he brakes. . . .

Your George

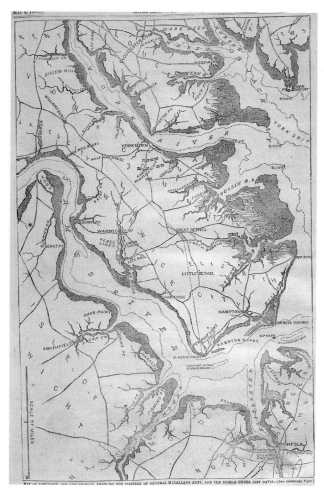

Map showing the positions of Union and Confederate troops around the lower James River in mid-April 1862. Harper's Weekly, *May 3, 1862.*
From the Collections of The Mariners' Museum.

Late on Wednesday, April 3, the quartermaster on watch was surprised to see a tiny rowboat pull alongside the *Monitor.* In it were an officer and a pair of "seedy looking men" at the oars. The officer was General McClellan, who had arrived at Fort Monroe the evening before to confer with the naval commanders at Hampton Roads about their ability to bottle up the *Virginia.* Expecting a ceremonial visit by the general, the *Monitor* crew had cleaned up. "You may imagine our officers were surprised to see him come in such a boat," Geer told his wife.[4]

The next afternoon the sailors on the deck of the *Monitor* heard the reverberation of field artillery as the lead elements of McClellan's army encountered the outnumbered Confederates under General "Prince John" Magruder, who made a show of much greater strength than he actually had. Magruder deliberately marched and countermarched his few thousand men one way and another before Yankee telescopes, and the guns Geer heard were aimed at those moving columns. A skirmish erupted as the Federals approached Confederate defenses along the Warwick River.

"I hear from shore this morning that our loss yesterday was 500 killed or wounded," wrote Geer, repeating exaggerated rumors of bloody strife that had floated out to the *Monitor*. In fact, fewer than fifty Union soldiers were dead or wounded.

In his letter of April 6 Geer refers to a message that the commander of the CSS *Virginia* relayed to Lieutenant Jeffers, of the *Monitor*, offering what amounted to a challenge. If such a message was delivered on paper, it did not survive to be recorded or mentioned in any official correspondence. On the very day that Geer wrote that letter, however, the top Confederate naval officers in Norfolk met to devise a plan for capturing the *Monitor* by boarding her, wedging the turret so it could not revolve, blinding the pilothouse with a shroud, and choking off the smokestack with wet blankets. Flag Officer Josiah Tattnall, Buchanan's successor, devised the plan, and McClellan's ascent of the peninsula escalated the stakes. The *Monitor* was all that really stood in the *Virginia*'s path to the York River, where the Confederate ship would have to go if it were to challenge McClellan's supply ships. Once McClellan made it past the batteries at Yorktown, there was nothing on the York that could interrupt Federal supplies.[5]

Hampton Roads, April 6, 1862

Dear Wife

. . . We are having very sturring times. Yesterday the Booming of Cannons could be heard all day in the direction of Yorktown and was renewed this morning. I hear from shore this morning that our loss yesterday was 500 Killed & Wounded. All the doctors that could be spared were sent out this morning and 5000 more Troops.

General McClelan is here in command. He come in on Thursday in the St[eam] Boat Comodore and Friday morning every thing on the Ship was put in the best of order and we watched every Steam Boat that came to us, expecting to see the Hero, but no hero came. 4 oclock arived and no General and he was given up for the day when an old row Boat came along side and an Officer came on Board and introduced himself as Genl McClelan. You may immagin our Officers were surprised to see him come in such a Boat. Yesterday the Flag of Truce brought down the compliments of the Captain of the Merimack to our Capt saying he should pay him a visit to day without fail, but he has not made his apierance yet, 12 oclock, and I think it is only brag and blow, although we were all night getting the Fires in the best of Order and we are keeping a good look out. It is a clear, beautiful day, and we can see Sewells Point very plain.

. . . We have received some new kinds of shells this week. They are filled with a liquid that takes fire when it Explodes and burns terrific. It will burn Woods or Ships, and the more water put on it the worse it Burns.

. . . I think as soon as McClellan takes Yorktown he will moove up the River and smoke out Mr Merimack and destroy the River Baterys.

Monday Morning, April 7

Yesterday we had to Coal Ship and I did not have a chance to finish this. It is a dirty job and every body has to help. . . .

Your Husband
George

At home in New York, Martha Geer had found a new apartment (on Allen Street) and announced that she would be moving on April 9. Her letter to her husband, which like all the others disappeared into a firebox on the *Monitor*, must have expressed the stress and fears of a cash-strapped wife undertaking the transfer of her household while her husband was away at war. In a telling reply, Geer hinted that he had begun to scheme for a way out of the navy:

"I think I have a plan by which I can get away from here when I get ready, and that will be as soon as I think there is any prospect of my getting any thing to do at home," he wrote. Yet, to him, Martha's fears were at odds with the already fabled account of *Monitor*'s clash with her Confederate foe.

"I see . . . that you have worked yourself into a regular stew about this ship being sunk, and the guns bursting, and us all being Drowned," he wrote on April 8, "but how can you believe such trash when we have been so severly tested. We will neaver have another so severe a battle; we were fighting some times with our Guns within 20 feet of each other. How can we fight any harder? Her Balls had no affect on us. You may not be aware that there is twenty one vessels of diferant discriptions wating here

> *You wish I was home.*
> *God knows I do, to, and*
> *my thoughts will be with*
> *you all day tomorrow.*
>
> — APRIL 8, 1862

for her, so you see we are not to do all the fighting nex time. The Vanderbilt & Arago are both here and have Steel Plating on their bows, and are both to run on the Merimack at once under a full head of Steam, and I have no doubt they are so large but what they will sink her. . . .

"A report came to us yesterday that the Merimack and 4 other Steamers were laying inside of Sewels Point and would come out as soon as the Storm Cleared away, but I have hearn so many storys about her that I do not believe any of them. . . ."

Before long, George Geer would be describing for Martha the first, frustrating encounter between the *Monitor* and the *Virginia* since the battle of March 9. In hopes of implementing his plan to capture the *Monitor*, Josiah Tattnall started his little fleet from Norfolk at 6:00 A.M. on April 11, parking the *Virginia* at the entrance to Hampton Roads with the little steamers *Raleigh* and *Jamestown* alongside. Across the way, several Union ships fired signal guns, and smaller

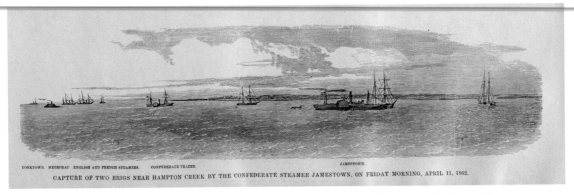

YORKTOWN. MERRIMAC. ENGLISH AND FRENCH STEAMERS. CONFEDERATE TEAZER. JAMESTOWN.
CAPTURE OF TWO BRIGS NEAR HAMPTON CREEK BY THE CONFEDERATE STEAMER JAMESTOWN, ON FRIDAY MORNING, APRIL 11, 1862.

"Capture of two brigs near Hampton Creek by the Confederate steamer Jamestown, *on Friday morning, April 11, 1862."*
COURTESY PICTORIAL BATTLES OF THE CIVIL WAR.

craft at the outer edge of the squadron scurried back to the protection of their larger sisters. Under the guns of Fort Monroe, drums aboard the Federal vessels beat their crews to quarters, and the *Monitor* moved out in front. Yet, given Flag Officer Louis Goldsborough's orders to avoid unnecessary risk, Lieutenant Jeffers refused to press on with the *Monitor* to the Confederate side. Tattnall clung to his own position, afraid of being cut off from Norfolk or having his boarding party annihilated by fire from other ships. The standoff lasted for hours. Finally Tattnall's contempt began to show. He sent the *Jamestown* across the river toward Hampton, in front of the enemy fleet, to cut out three little coasters. Even that failed to taunt the Yankees to action, and that afternoon Tattnall finally pulled back in disgust.[6]

The Confederate officer was not the only one dissatisfied.

". . . We have been very much provoked for the last two days by the Merimack," Geer wrote on April 13. "She comes down in the Roads in plain sight but under cover of Sewels Point Batery and lays there as much as to dare us to atack her, but our own orders are such that we cannot go after her, but must lay here like an old coward and look at her. One of her consorts, the Jamestown, ran over by Hampton and cut out three Schooners right under our nose when a fiew shot from us would have sunk her, but our orders are so strict we cannot make a moove unless the Comodore signalizes us to. If ever a man was cursed I think that Comodore Golesborrow has been by our Crew for the last two days."

Cannon fire that Geer supposed to be part of a "terrific Battle" consisted of routine siege operations around Yorktown. Not even a skirmish was reported that day.

The Monitor Chronicles

Dear Wife

. . . How strange it seams to me: I cannot realise you have mooved. The idea—that I will not go home to Pitt St. when I get on shore but will go looking along Allen st. to find where my Wife lives. If I do not find the house (you know I will be very strange when I get back), I will have to advertise for a lost Wife and two little kidds.

. . . We have been very much provoked for the last two days by the Merimack. She comes down in the Roads in plain sight but under cover of Sewels Point Batery and lays there as much as to dare us to atack her, but our own orders are such that we cannot go after her, but must lay here like an old coward and look at her. One of her consorts, the Jamestown, ran over by Hampton and cut out three Schooners right under our nose when a fiew shot from us would have sunk her, but our orders are so strict we cannot make a moove unless the Comodore signalizes us to. If ever a man was cursed I think that Comodore Golesborrow has been by our Crew for the last two days.

    We lay about two miles in advance of the rest of the ships and I am satisfied the Merimack is afraid of us, or she would make an atack on us. I had a good look at her yesterday through a Spy Glass. She is very large and I could see a great many men on her roof, or Deck. . . .

    We can hear heavy Cannonading in the direction of Yorktown; there must be a terrific Battle going on up there.

    . . . Dont fail to write me long Lettors. Kiss both Babys for me.

Your Husband
George

The hours of tension between the ironclads barely broke the tedium of duty aboard the idle *Monitor*. As days passed, gunfire once again echoed all the way from Hampton Roads. At Lee's Mill, some twenty miles away, Confederate forces were engaged in a skirmish with a Union division reconnoitering across the Warwick River. A Vermont brigade suffered about 150 casualties, and as the largest action yet in the Peninsula Campaign it earned undue attention. It would soon pale in comparison to the massive clashes closer to Richmond.[7]

As always, the sound of siege operations around Yorktown echoed as far away as Hampton Roads. Reluctant to waste his troops in frontal assaults, George McClellan dragged his heavy guns up from Fort Monroe and carefully placed them before the Confederate entrenchments. He expended more than three weeks of his campaign in the reduction of that thinly defended line. The delay allowed the enemy to transfer its main army from northern Virginia to Richmond and the threatened peninsula.

———

"Dear Wife," began George Geer's letter of April 16. ". . . I have been wating so anctiously for this Lettor of yours; I have been morose and have hardly spoken to any one since Sunday, but now I feel like myself again."

Geer was as homesick as ever. He shunned the traditional alcoholic remedies for melancholy—liquid solace that landed less temperate shipmates in irons and helped to put the *Monitor* off limits to most visitors.

". . . Frank Loomis was here to see me and I took him through the Ship," Geer wrote. "It was a privlage a great many try to get, but fiew succeed now, as they have stoped the stream of visitors as there was

> *... How we all hope and pray that Capt. Worden may come back to us. There is not one on the ship among the Officers or men but hate the Captain; he is a regular old growler, always finding fault. I wish he would fall overboard. He mint [might] go to the bottom for all the help I would give him.*

— APRIL 21, 1862

to many of our men Drunk. They would get Liquor some way, and nobody could tell how. The first Lieutenant had the vesil surched, and found considerable Whiskey hid away, and nobody knew where they got it."

All around him, miscreants were suffering at the hands of the unforgiving Lieutenant Jeffers:

". . . There is a Saylor laying on the floor under my feet with Irons on his Hands and Feet; his hands are behind his back, and he has been in that shape for three days and will have to stay so untill Saturday. Two Saylors got in a fight to day and they are on deck with their hand[s] Ironed behind each others back so that they are hugging each other, and perhaps they will have to stay so for three or four days, but it is good enough for them. I am completely disgusted with Saylors, and have no pity for them. They do not seam to know anything but Whores and Rum, and it is about all you hear them talk about. I have but very little to do with them. . . ."

His letters from this period show Geer asking his wife for news of Congress passing a personal bankruptcy law—a sign of how far his economic fortunes had sunk. They also show him learning how cramped and comfortless a home the little *Monitor* could be. A long, rainy April weekend confined officers and crew to the interior of the ship. Despite their relative comforts, officers grumbled as steadily as the enlisted men who endured their confinement in a cluster on the berth deck.[8]

The bad weather also foretold the vulnerability of the *Monitor* to any but the calmest seas. "We have been housed up here sence Friday," wrote Geer on April 21. "It has rained and blowed steady all the time, and the waves wash over us so it [is] most imposeable to stand on Deck, and our Hatches

The Monitor Chronicles

54

fit so poorly they let the water down in torants, and I have been wett as [a] sop for three days, but I am wett so much I do not mind it and have not had a Cold sence I left New York."

U.S. Steamer Monitor
Hampton Roads, Apr 21, 1862

. . . Your Lettor of Wednesday should have been here on Friday [*but*] has not arived yet. It may come before I close this, as We expect the Mail every moment. If not, I shall feel very disapointed.

We have been housed up here sence Friday. It has rained and blowed steady all the time, and the waves wash over us so it [*is*] most imposeable to stand on Deck, and our Hatches fit so poorly they let the water down in torants, and I have been wett as [*a*] sop for three days, but I am wett so much I do not mind it and have not had a Cold sence I left New York.

. . . Every day we can hear heavy firing from the direction of Yorktown. I suppose when the fight commences in good earnest we will hear it very plain.

I am very glad the time is drawing near when you will be able to get that money, so you can be a little indipendant.

How we all hope and pray that Capt. Worden may come back to us. There is not one on the ship among the Officers or men but hate the Captain; he is a regular old growler, always finding fault. I wish he would fall overboard. He mint [*might*] go to the bottom for all the help I would give him.

Your Lettor has this moment come to hand, with one from Johney. The delay . . . was caused by you not putting a one cent stamp on, and I have to pay three cents— or rather get the Purcer to trust me, as I did not have the money.

I will answer your Lettor nex time. Dont make a mistake about the stamps again.

Yours in Haste
George

THE STANDOFF

As the *Monitor* languished, her crew's contempt for Lieutenant Jeffers was steadily growing, feeding their regard for the absent Worden, whom they all expected to be sent back to his former post. Their affection for their wounded captain finally found expression in a letter composed, apparently, by one of the enlisted men, who signed it from the entire crew. Headed April 24, it was addressed to "our Dear and Honered Captain."

"These few lines," the letter read, "is from your own Crew of the *Monitor* with there Kindest Love to you[,] there Honered Captain[,] Hoping to God that they will have the pleasure of Welcoming you back to us again Soon. . . . [S]ince you left us we have had no pleasure on Board of the *Monitor*. . . ." The homely memorial ended with the promise that "We Remain untill Death your Affectionate Crew, The Monitor Boys."

Worden opened the envelope in his Washington bedroom a few days later. If he was amused by the crude delivery, he was touched by the sentiments. Endorsing the page with the details of its receipt, he filed it with his personal papers.

At 3:00 P.M. on the same day this letter was written, another ironclad Union warship dropped anchor off Fort Monroe. The USS *Galena*, a more conventional, propeller-driven steamer, longer than the *Monitor* but more lightly armored, had come down from the Brooklyn Navy Yard. She arrived with engine trouble, but once repaired she was expected to add considerably to the Union's naval strength at the mouths of the James and York rivers. The *Galena* carried two nine-inch Dahlgren smoothbore guns, smaller than the pair on the *Monitor*, but she also sported a couple of Parrott hundred-pounder rifles that offered much greater penetrating power. Fireman Geer scanned the thinner sheathing of the new gunboat's sides, though, and accurately predicted that she would stand little chance against a real ironclad.[9]

U.S. Steamer Monitor
Hampton Roads, Apr 27/62

Dear Wife

. . . The wonderfull Galena has arived, but she is not much account. The Merimack would make very short work of her; her own men have very little confidence in her, and would be very glad of the chance to get on here. . . .

. . . We have had a general Muster this morning. My cloaths looked rather rusty; I shall have to draw Shirt, Shoes, and Cap the first of the month, then I will be able to look quite respectible on Muster.

. . . I shall know how to pity you on Wash day in future. There is nothing I hate so bad as to have to wash my Cloathing. I put them to soak in a pail and hide them for a week and then take them and give them a little rub and squese and ring them out. I dont think they look any <u>Whiter than yourn</u> do.

. . . If you could see how I am writting this you would not expect a very long one. I am on the Hammocks, where I cannot sett up strait and can hardly move my arms.

Your Husband
George

By the end of April, Martha was finally able to begin drawing her allotment of Geer's wages. Now Geer's thoughts could turn to another unsatisfied element of their separation—sex. His letter of April 30 contains one blatantly un-Victorian remark. The manuscript version of this letter is missing from the surviving collection, and is available only in the transcripts that accompanied the originals. The transcriber took numerous liberties with spelling, punctuation, and syntax, but (except for a few words that Geer habitually misspelled), it is the text of the transcript that appears here.

U.S.S. Monitor
Hampton Roads
April 30, 1862

Dear Wife

. . . I am very much surprised to hear of the increase in Mr. Walkers family. He does not have very good luck trying to get a boy, but he will have to do as I am going to do—to get a girl, that is, keep trying. I think if I do not see you for six months I shall be able to make a girl or a pair of boys, so look out for me.

. . . You dont say any thing about the little ones. Do put in one line about them. Dont tell me any thing about shad or any thing else good to eat, or you will make my guts think my throat is cut. We have very fine Oysters along side every day. Those that have money buy them, but I have the fun of looking at them eating them.

But I dont care for any thing if I can get that chocolate and milk to have when I go on watch at night.

Geer depended on his wife to mail him crucial items that he could not obtain aboard ship—stamps, writing paper, envelopes, and the occasional newspaper. For a time she sent him letters tucked inside the *Mercury* to save postage, but when he learned that she risked a $250 fine he advised her to send only items that could not be traced to her as the source.

It was now two months into George Geer's stint aboard the *Monitor*—sixty mostly sedentary days punctuated by only one real encounter with the enemy. He hungered for more action, in part because he wanted the war to end so he could go home. Spring had begun to give way to the often grueling hot and humid Virginia summer. On May 3 his mood erupted into an impatient mix of irritation and wishful thinking.

Hampton Roads, May 3, 1862

. . . I am very much surprised, and shall be very much provoked if you have sent me a box by the Navy Yard. I do not understand wheather you are going to send it [*at*] once, or not untill you hear from me. I <u>do not want</u> you to send me any Box untill I tell you, and that will not be untill I am satisfied you can spare the money and I want it sent only by Express. If you was to send it by the Navy I would not get it in three months, if at all.

I shall look for a supply of Writting Paper and Envelopes from you in the Mercury. I want you to send me in next Sundays Mercury, if you have it to spair, a piece of Casteel Soap. This Soap, the saylors say, will make sore Eyes, and I dont want them.

You say you do not take the Papers. When you commence to get money, so you can say you have two cents over, buy a Paper, for there is something about us or the Merimack most every day. She has not shown her self lately, and I have very little fear of her. I am satisfied she is afraid of us, and we will not get a shot at her again untill we go after her.

. . . We had some Officers here yesterday from Burnsides Army. They report that Savannah has been captured, so you see the Rebelion is fast drawing to a close, and I believe I can get my discharge from the Navy in less than Six months. . . .

Your Husband
George S. Geer

The arrival of staff officers from General Ambrose Burnside's army on the coast of North Carolina and the exaggerated news of the fall of Fort Pulaski, near Savannah, hinted at an early conclusion to the war. Burnside had had little but success in his Carolina campaign, and with his old friend McClellan it seemed they could not fail to wind up the little drama. And while excitement did await the *Monitor* crew in the following week, Geer's prediction of a November discharge fell short by more than three years.

Dear Wife
                                    I have received
I wrote you last the Papers on the
and Times and to day the Times an
ever welcom Letter The Locks came safe
but I do not understand why you
ballance of them & in the Times an
you sent them before you left
much pleased to hear you are
hope you will have a very
there and I suppose you will g
a visit at least I hope you wi
would be very glad to see you
you first rate When you hav
how long you are going to st
will know how long to direc
and if you are going to Oran
home I suppose you will
soon as Rachel to take care of
would go to Troy with Willey
Willey could see his

Three

THE RIVER

MᴄCʟᴇʟʟᴀɴ'ꜱ ꜱᴛᴀʟʟᴇᴅ ᴄᴀᴍᴘᴀɪɢɴ once again geared up on May 3, when the Confederates evacuated Yorktown. The next day, McClellan's advance began sparring with them near Williamsburg. On May 5, after a little battle that cost far fewer lives than Geer understood, the Union army moved into the old colonial capital and General Joe Johnston's army fled toward Richmond.

That left Norfolk isolated from military support. Threatened by Burnside's forces to the south, the Confederate army started moving its equipment and supplies out of the city. A similar process began across the Elizabeth River, at the navy yard, which was facing the torch for the second time in barely a year. The evacuation of matériel began in earnest as soon as the news of Yorktown and Willamsburg arrived, but Union forces around Hampton Roads remained still for a couple of days.

As these events unfolded, the *Monitor* lay quietly at anchor. George Geer and the rest of the engineer department kept busy, and grimy, installing a new pump to counteract the ship's proven propensity for taking on water, as well as to provide against injuries to the hull from ramming. They interrupted their week's toil on May 6 to greet a special visitor—Abe Lincoln.

U.S. Steamer Monitor
Hampton Roads, Apr [May] 7, 1862

Dear Wife

. . . We are putting in a Steam Pump and two Engines to drive it . . . in case we get a hole in our side . . . It will pump 2500 Gallons pr minnit. It will keep us afloat if the hole was large enough for me to crall through. . . .

We are forbid by the Navy Department from Writting any thing regarding the moovement of Ships, but I am going to write you all I know. This morning at Seven the Galena and two Gun Boats started up the James River towards Richmond. They had not got out of sight when a small Steam Boat came out of the Elizabeth River and Steamed over for Newport News. They soon came down to the Fort and say they ran away from Norfolk this morning and that the Rebels are deserting Norfolk.

The President was here yesterday and was very much pleased with the looks of our craft. Our Boat has just come from shore and says that the President has sent for the Comodore, and thinks we will be ordered up to Norfolk this Afternoon to prevent the Rebels from distroying the Navy Yard and other property. I hope I will get your next Lettor there. Our men are wild with excitement and will be very much put out if we do not go up there.

Anticipating significant movements with the capture of Yorktown, President Lincoln had boarded a revenue cutter with two members of his cabinet and steamed down to Fort Monroe for a personal view of the operations. He reviewed the naval forces first, boarding the *Minnesota* and then the big *Vanderbilt*, with its new subsurface ram for paunching the *Virginia*. Next, the distinguished party steamed around the *Naugatuck*—an armored steamer with one great rifled gun that was also called the *Stevens Battery*, after the man who built the ship and donated it to the government—and the *Monitor*. The towering chief executive came aboard, shook a few hands, and gave the impression that he thought the little iron tub quite a ship. The crew mustered on deck, and Lincoln doffed his black stovepipe as he strode before them.

Lincoln's presence at Hampton Roads helped budge Flag Officer Goldsborough, whose age and obesity may have contributed to the lethargic military activity there. The president asked Goldsborough to send three gunboats upriver to help clear McClellan's way, and on the morning of May 8 the *Galena* led two other steamers up the James. Virtually across their wake came a tug from Norfolk at full steam, steered by a loyal captain who headed first for Newport News and then for the fort, where he reported that the Confederates were abandoning Norfolk.[1]

At Lincoln's behest, Goldsborough ordered his fleet to move against Norfolk's outpost at Sewell's Point on May 8. Just after noon, six ships mounting a total of forty-one guns moved out from Old Point Comfort. Five of them anchored a couple of miles off Sewell's Point and began shelling at long range, while the *Monitor* moved in to a mile's distance. The outermost battery on the point ceased firing after a brief pounding, and the Union vessels turned their guns on another fort farther inland. Several hours later, the *Monitor* turned back toward her sisters, but then smoke appeared over the treetops beyond Sewell's Point. It was the

I suppose you see by the Papers that McClellan is pushing on toward Richmond. I hear from Shore this morning that yesterday they had a very hard fight and our loss was about 2000 Killed, but we whiped them. I think I am very fortunate I am in the Navy in place of the army. . . . The Letters are going on Shore and I must close. Give my Love to all hand[s].

— MAY 7, 1862

exhaust of a vessel steaming up the Elizabeth River. In fact, it was the *Virginia*, come alone to confront Norfolk's assailants.

The wooden Union gunboats scampered back to Fort Monroe, but the *Monitor* and the *Naugatuck* stood by to engage the Confederate titan. The *Virginia* was not there for pitched battle, however—unless the Yankees tried to ascend the Elizabeth. And at that moment, the U.S. Navy was not interested in going up that river. The damage they had inflicted on the Sewell's Point batteries was satisfaction enough. So, as much as the big ironclad flaunted herself, no

Engraving showing the relative positions of Hampton Roads sites such as Fortress Monroe, Old Point Comfort, and Sewell's Point. <small>Courtesy Junior League of Hampton Roads.</small>

opponent took up the challenge. After a time, Goldsborough signaled his ships back home, and the *Virginia* slid back to Sewell's Point and rattled down her anchor.[2]

The next morning Abraham Lincoln himself came alongside the *Monitor* and hailed Lieutenant Jeffers for permission to come aboard. Evidently dissatisfied with Goldsborough's energy, or lack of it, the president wished to know if it would be appropriate for him to order Jeffers across the roadstead for a little reconnaissance of Sewell's Point. Jeffers was not about to question an order from the commander in chief, but he asked Lincoln to inform Goldsborough of it beforehand. Then the *Monitor* glided across to find that the enemy had abandoned the point.

With this information, the president grew impatient for more action. He spurred Major General John Wool, the septuagenarian commander of Fort Monroe, to land troops on the other side, and that afternoon Wool began preparing two brigades for the crossing. The next morning Wool landed the division on the undefended Chesapeake Bay side of Willoughby's Point and came at Norfolk from the east. In the company of the secretary of the treasury, General Wool rode to the city limits, where the mayor of

"The Mayor & Councils of
Norfolk meeting the federal
forces under a flag of truce."
Engraving from Harper's
Weekly, May 24, 1862.
FROM THE COLLECTIONS OF
THE MARINERS' MUSEUM.

Norfolk met him and surrendered the city, beyond which rose an ominous plume of dark smoke.

⁘

The only hope for the *Virginia* lay in an escape up the James River under cover of darkness. The *Patrick Henry* and *Jamestown* had slipped out the night of May 6, towing the unfinished ironclad *Richmond* up the river toward its namesake city, but the *Virginia* had a deeper draft. The pilots insisted they could guide the ram far up the James if the vessel could be lightened, reducing her draft to a depth of eighteen feet. In the darkness Flag Officer Tattnall set his crew to throwing overboard everything that could be spared. Soon, the ship floated higher—so high that her unprotected wooden hull peeked above the surface. Now, however, the wind shifted and the pilots began to balk, re-ducing their estimate of the upriver distance the *Virginia* could achieve to so little that the now-vulnerable ship could not escape the enemy on shore. Having burned his bridges, and knowing that he had at least three powerful gunboats to face on the James, for Tattnall the options were clear. Rather than lose her to the enemy, he chose to destroy the *Virginia*. Fires kindled fore and aft in the wee hours of May 11 reached the magazine just before dawn, and the pride of the Confederate navy settled into shallow water just south of Craney Island.[3]

⁘

Over on the Union side of the roads, George Geer heard the explosion that announced the demise of the mighty *Merrimack*. Within six hours, the *Monitor* lay before fabled Norfolk, the first Union vessel into the city.

THE RIVER

Dear Wife

You see by the heading of this Lettor that we are at last at the much talked of Norfolk, and the great Monster Merimack is no more. . . .

On Thursday morning we received orders to go up and shell the Batery on Sewels Point. We started at Seven and were at work by 9 oclock. We went up clost to the Dock in front of the Batery and threw Eighteen of our Incindiary Shels, setting the works on fire. We then steamed away about half mile and let the other Gun Boats (of which there were five with us) do the work of shelling them out while they were trying to put the fire out. It was fun to see the Shell explode in and around the Works.

One Shot from the Semanole cared [carried] their Flag away and we could see several Rebels trying to put one up again when another shell struck them and they disapiered very soon— probably not to serve Jef [Davis] any longer.

After we had silenced all their Baterys the Merimack was seen coming down. All the other Ships started at once, and I thought we would shurly have a fight with her, but as she came towards us we kept going towards the Fort. Our Captain said his orders were not to fight her alone, but get her out in Hampton Roads. She was to smart for us, and only came down as far as Crany Island and laid there, so we went back to our old anchorage.

Friday we had the President on board, and he gave us Orders to go and reconorter Sewels Point, and if the Merimack came for our Captain to use his own judgment about atacking her. We went over and found Sewels Point was deserted, and wated all day to see if the old devil would come out, but she would not come so we had to go back again, disapointed.

Yesterday a large body of Troops were mooved forward, towards Norfolk, and this morning about 4 oclock a very large Explosion took place and nothing could be seen of the Merimack after it, so we had orders to moove at once to Norfolk. But what was our disapointment to learn, as [*we*] were leaving, that the Troops had taken Norfolk at 5 oclock last evening. So we started on, and the rest of the vesels followed us, and by 10 oclock we were laying in front of Norfolk. The Rebels have distroyed every thing at the Navy Yard, and blew up the dry Dock.

I think the People are all sesesh here, as there is not a Union Flag to be seen. We have just cast off and are on our way down to Hampton Roads to get some coal, and tomorrow morning we start for Richmond.

This Postage Stamp I got from a boy who came along side of us at Norfolk. He had some Bills of the Southern Confed, but as I had no money I could not get one from him.

. . . I did not get over 4 hours sleep any night last week, and feel pretty well used up and have a prospect of working most of the night Coaling Ship. I will write you from Richmond.

George

Geer was very nearly correct when he told his wife that he would write her next from Richmond. What was left of the Confederate navy fled upriver to the fortified bluffs just below that city. Meanwhile, the *Monitor* took on coal through the next night, in quick preparation for a cruise up the James. When the order came to start upriver, the ironclad departed with its pantry only partly stocked. Paymaster Keeler had underestimated how long it would take to process his requests for supplies. With skimpy provisions, the *Monitor* and the one-gun *Naugatuck* churned around Newport News Point together before dawn on May 12, with orders to meet the *Galena* and two wooden companions at Jamestown Island.

Keeler wasn't alone in failing to understand his duties. To assure that defenseless storeships could pass safely upriver to resupply the Union gunboats, Flag Officer Goldsborough had instructed Lieutenant Jeffers to stop at each Confederate battery on the James, shell it into submission, and go ashore with a party to spike the guns and fire the magazines. Instead, when enemy cannon opened on the two armored vessels that afternoon, Jeffers ordered the helm turned for the relative safety of the far side of the river. With fewer than sixty officers and crew, he might have been loath to risk skirmishes on land, but his failure to even make an attempt threw Goldsborough into a rage. The little fleet had been embarrassed.

That afternoon the ironclads made their rendezvous with the *Galena, Aroostook,* and *Port Royal,* within sight of the island where John Smith had located the first Virginia colony two and a half centuries before. Lieutenant Jeffers presumably conveyed to the captain of the *Galena,* Commander John Rodgers, Goldsborough's wish that they steam up to Richmond—"if possible, without any unnecessary delay"—and beat the city into surrender. At 4:00 A.M. the next morning, the five ships started upstream again. They crept along unmolested all day, and on the third morning they passed a plantation dock known as Harrison's Landing, where the Army of the Potomac would come to ignominious rest seven weeks hence.

Several miles upriver from Harrison's Landing lay City Point, where the Appomattox River spilled into the James. Smoke curled up from the point, where retreating Confederates had burned the depot. The little flotilla stopped here for a few hours, but continued on that

"Harrison's Landing, on the James River, the new base of the Army of the Potomac." Engraving from Harper's Weekly, *July 19, 1862.* FROM THE COLLECTIONS OF THE MARINERS' MUSEUM.

HARRISON'S LANDING, ON THE JAMES RIVER, THE NEW BASE OF THE ARMY OF THE POTOMAC.

afternoon; Rodgers had every intention of following Goldsborough's instructions, even if it meant attacking Richmond with five little ships bearing twenty guns and fewer than five hundred men.

A runaway slave joined the fleet as it wound around the hairpin loops of the river above the mouth of the Appomattox. He warned that the Confederates had a massive battery at Drewry's Bluff, eight miles below Richmond, so that evening Commander Rodgers stopped at Kingsland Creek, about three miles short of the bluff.

The next morning the *Monitor* again encountered the crew of the *Virginia*, which had traveled to Richmond by train only to find that the guns at Drewry's Bluff needed gunners. The *Galena* led the way that day between narrowing riverbanks infested with aggravatingly accurate marksmen. One Southern sharpshooter picked off the leadsman on the *Galena*, and others sent bullets whistling between Paymaster Keeler's knees and over Lieutenant Greene's head as the pair stood atop the turret.[4] Chief Engineer Stimers no longer rode the *Monitor*, having returned to his duties as a naval inspector, and that had led to an upward shuffle in the ironclad's engineer department. George Geer took control of the engine levers this May 15, thus standing to the post of a third assistant engineer—the commissioned grade to which he aspired.

⁓

Sunken hulks blocked the channel at Drewry's Bluff, and there the numerous batteries poured their fire into the squadron, riddling the *Galena*. The *Aroostook* and *Port Royal* dared not venture close with their wooden hulls, so the *Naugatuck* and *Monitor* steamed up to help the flagship. The hundred-pounder Parrott rifle on the *Naugatuck* burst, injuring one gunner in the process and leaving that little craft unarmed. Only the *Monitor* could stand the shelling, but when she moved in close Lieutenant Greene found that he could not raise his gun muzzles enough to reach the bluffs. Jeffers dropped back so the gunners could find the elevation.

As the fight wore on, the interior of the *Monitor* grew unbearably warm. It had been oppressively hot outside for days, and more heat from the boilers and gun tubes took the mercury soaring to well over a hundred degrees. Jeffers guessed that it was 140 degrees inside the turret. Sulfur fumes from the gunpowder, coal gas drifting up from the engine room, and smoke from the lanterns combined with the heat and humidity to weaken the gun crews. Several of the sturdiest in the gun crew collapsed, and so many men grew faint that Jeffers withdrew from the contest for fifteen minutes so the gunners could go down to the berth deck and inhale less contaminated air.

After more than three hours of daunting fire, the *Galena* ran out of ammunition and

Rodgers signaled a retreat back to Kingsland Creek. The *Galena* had lost two dozen men, of whom thirteen had been killed outright.[5]

Isaac Newton, now acting as chief engineer for the *Monitor*, complimented Geer on his performance during the fight, and the ambitious fireman beamed appreciatively. Knowing that his wife would worry about him when she read of the battle, Geer wrote her about it almost as soon as the firing had stopped. His account of the expedition reads as well, if not as clearly, as those of his superiors.

U.S. Steamer Monitor, 8 Miles
from Richmond, May 15, 1862

Dear Wife

We have been fighting all day and have come off 2nd best. . . . We commenced Coaling as soon as we arived in the Roads, and it was most morning before we finished, and at foor oclock we started up James River to help the Galena and the two other Boats to fight their way to Richmond. About 10 oclock we met two steamboats flying the Rebel Rag coming, aparently, streight on to us. Our Guns was loaded with Grape and A[i]med, ready for the word to fire, when our pilot called out that it was a flag of truce. We left the Guns and went on deck, and when they passed us we gave them some harty chears, as there was several hundred union prisoners on their way to the forte to be exchanged. Our Captain felt very much rejoyced to to [sic] think he did not give the word to our gunners to fire, as we should have slaughtered many of our own poor fellows.

We steamed on untill 2 oclock, when a Rebel Batry opened on us, but the Captain did not think it worth fireing at, as the River was wide enough for us to keep out of their way. I did not think to say that the Naugituck was with us all the time.

About three oclock we came up with the Galena, Roostick, &

Port Royal. . . . We all lay at anchor untill the next morning at 4 oclock, when we all got under way and started up the river, expecting to meet some Batery about thirty miles up the River, but when we came to them we found them deserted, so we did not wate but put on some miles beyond to a good anchorage and Anchored for the night.

Wednesday morning we started again at day light and about noon we saw a very large smoke some two miles in advance of us. Our pilot said it was City Point. When we got to it we found it was the Depot building. . . . The Cars had left with all the troops on and set the building on fire before they started. The Road runs to Petersburg and Richmond.

The U.S. military railroad depot building, City Point, Virginia, as it looked in 1864 in this U.S. Army Signal Corps photograph. FROM THE COLLECTIONS OF THE MARINERS' MUSEUM.

There was very few white people left there, but what there were all had the white flag flying. There was one Union White Woman who refused to leve and came on Board of the Galena and gave Captain Rogers a Petersburg Paper which had an account of the distruction of the Merimack. They were very bitter against Jef Davis for Blowing her up.

We . . . left City Point and steamed up to here and found out by a Niger who came on Board that there was a very strong Fort some two miles above, so we Anchored for the night. Soon after anchoring we spide a lot of Rebel Sharp Shooters skulking along the shore, but they did not come clost enough to do any damage. We all—that is,

> *The Rebel sharp Shooters are firing at us all the time. None of us are alowed to go on deck, and I can assure you I am not going to risk my self where there is any danger if I can help it, for what is the Cuntry worth to a man when his Wife is a Widdow?*
>
> — MAY 15, 1862

all the Ships—sent a gard of Pickets on shore and keep them there watching all the night, but they did not show them selves and this morning at day light the Pickets were called in, and soon after it was all a mans life was worth to go on deck. Every body was kept below, and the Roostick & Port Royal opened fire with their Howitsers and kept firing untill we were all ordered to moove forward and attack the Batery. The Galena, being the Flag ship, took the lead, and all the other ships followed her. It was necessary to keep a man throwing the Lead all the time, for fear they had filled up the River, and we had hardley started when their Sharp Shooters shot the man that was throwing the Lead on the Galena. Another man was put in his place and they soon picked him off, so the Ships all commenced to shell the Banks as we went along, and in that manner got with in range of the Forts.

When the hot work commenced in good earness we found in place of one Fort that there was any quantity of them, and worse than all, the Galena prooved a perfect falure and we were the only Boat that could get up clost to them. But they could have fought us for a week, as we, you know, have but two Guns while the Rebels had Guns as large as ours and any quantity of them, so it would be useless for us to fight them alone.

The Galena prooved no bettor than a Wooden vesel. Every shot kept going through her sides. I was on deck before I commenced to write, and I could count 17 Holes in her side as she lays near us. Our Boat has just come from her, and the men say there is 7 Killed and 20 Wounded. Our Doctor has gone to her to help dress the wounded. I am glad I was not on her; I dont think there will be any more Galenas built.

We were only struck 3 times. They seamed to know it was no use to fire at us, but we did not think so about them, as we kept a poring the shot in them as fast as we could.

Sence I commenced this Lettor we have got under way and are steaming down to City Point, where we will wate untill one of our vesels go down to Hampton Roads after moore Gun Boats. . . .

I am writting this in hopes of sending it by the Port Royal, as I hear she leves for the Fort to night for reinforcements. The reason we are going down to City Point is not that we are running away, but there is a narow place in the Channel there, and we are afraid they will bring Schooners out from Petersburg and sink [them], so as to keep us from going down by that means. They would have us in [a] trap, but we are not going to give them a chance unless they have already done it, and you may know they have not if you receve this Lettor. You must not worey if you do not receive Lettors regular now, as we have to trust to chances to send a Lettor.

The Rebel sharp Shooters are firing at us all the time. None of us are alowed to go on deck, and I can assure you I am not going to risk my self where there is any danger if I can help it, for what is the Cuntry worth to a man when his Wife is a Widdow?

. . . Our Paymaster is a new man and Green, and he did not make out his requisition for stores untill too late to get them before we left; the result has been that we are out of shugar and have had to use Molasses to Sweeten our Tea & Coffee. We are out of Molasses to day and shall have to go with out any sweetening, and worse than all our Ships Bread, or Crackers, have all got moldy and sower, so we are living rather poor for me. Still, I do not grumble half as much as these damd English—of which we have some 8 or 10 in our crew who, I dont believe, ever lived so well in their lives, or ever had enough to eat before they came here. . . .

Our Doctor has come back from the Galena and he says there is Sixteen killed. I think she is rather a poor speciman of Iron Clad. . . . I hear that there was one man Shot on the Naugituck.

This is a most beautiful River, and there is some very fine Plantations on it. I shall Learn something about the country on this Cruse.

Your Husband
George

From Kingsland Creek the ships fell back to City Point. The disabled *Naugatuck* returned to Hampton Roads, and Goldsborough came upriver with a tug and four more gunboats to subdue the batteries that Lieutenant Jeffers had ignored. Then he sent the ten-gun steam sloop *Wachusett* and three of the others ahead under Commander William Smith, to reinforce Rodgers. Because Smith outranked Rodgers, he superseded him at the head of the City Point squadron—but it was a command he would not hold for long.

With the banks on either side infested with enemy infantry, each ship's captain posted a heavy watch at night. No vessel lay more closely guarded than the *Monitor*, which had no freeboard to slow a boarding

"Rendezvous of our fleet in James River, off City Point." Engraving from Harper's Weekly, *June 21, 1862.* FROM THE COLLECTIONS OF THE MARINERS' MUSEUM.

party in boats. By day, patrols that resembled excursion parties went ashore. On the morning of May 19, Commander Smith took a jaunt ashore at City Point, where white flags signaled the surrender of its residents. Visiting door to door, he encountered two sick women, each in her own house and each complaining that she could find no doctor to treat her. Smith promised to send his ship's surgeon, and that afternoon he did. The captain's gig pulled ashore with eight men at the oars, the coxswain, the surgeon, and four other officers intending to

The Monitor Chronicles

play tourist in a Confederate town. The surgeon and three of the officers, including an army Signal Corps lieutenant who may have been sizing up the landscape for official purposes, went to find the ailing women, accompanied by five sailors. All carried cutlasses and navy revolvers. An hour later Keeler arrived at the landing in a second boat, on no other mission than to stretch his legs.

None of the *Monitor* visitors knew that, out of sight, two Georgia infantry detachments were just then changing places on the picket line. Earlier one of those pickets had furtively watched Commander Smith as he made his tour of the settlement. Now, though, the Confederate officers quickly conspired to bag both boatloads of Yankees. Members of the 22nd Georgia stalked the party ashore while a captain from the 4th Georgia led his men to the riverbank and demanded the surrender of the remaining boat's crew. The surgeon and his escort gave up without drawing a weapon.

Meanwhile, a slave had rushed down the bluff to warn the Union boats' crews. Keeler raced for his boat and leaped in, ordering his men to their oars and shouting a warning to the *Wachusett*'s boat. The Georgia captain soon reached the landing, but Master's Mate

Thomas Almy had shoved off and now refused to surrender, directing his men to put their backs into the escape. The Georgians opened fire, killing Almy and a seaman and seriously wounding three more sailors. One lone uninjured man finished the long pull back to the *Wachusett*, while the *Monitor* steamed up to offer help.

The ironclad threw a round of canister into a brick warehouse at the landing, but it was already too late. The prisoners had all been marched to Confederate headquarters, and the Georgians fell back out of sight. Still, the *Monitor* sent two incendiary shells through Appomattox Manor, the plantation home of the Eppes family, at the mouth of the Appomattox River. The shells failed to explode inside the structure, and its inhabitants came out in a boat to beg for their home.

Commander Smith corresponded with the Confederate commander, Benjamin Huger (the erstwhile army chief of Norfolk), but Huger would not recognize the humanitarian mission of so large an armed party. The prisoners remained prisoners, and the secretary of the navy blamed Smith, demoting him from command of the eight-ship division and sending him back to Hampton Roads to captain a smaller steamer.[6]

THE RIVER

77

Martha Geer read of the skirmish in a New York newspaper shortly after receiving George's letter of May 20, and so little did she understand the distinction between the seamen of a ship's deck crew and the fire-men and engineers of a steamer's engine crew that she supposed her husband might have been among the captured or wounded oarsmen of the gig. Geer set her straight in a subsequent letter, trying once again to ease her persistent fears, but now he had bigger news, both to deliver and digest. His steady performance had won him a choice position, but news from Troy overshadowed that promotion. A fire had apparently lev-eled every building his father owned there, leaving the elder Geer with neither a home nor rental income, and the sons who worked for him were left homeless by the same blaze.

U.S. Steamer Monitor
City Point, Va., May 20, 1862

Dear Wife

. . . We came down here and droped anchor on Friday. None of the Enemy were to be seen, and the people on shore told us there were none of them there, but we put no confidence in what they say and keep so far from shore that their sharp Shooters cannot reach us. In the action I acted as third Engineer, and was stationed at the reversing and Cut off Levers, and the Chief, Mr. Newton, said that the Engine was neaver worked so well before: quite a compliment for me.

On Sunday we were all dressed in our best, setting on deck, and I was thinking of you, and wondering if you were busy cleaning up, and if you found as much to do on Sunday morning as you used [to] when I was home, and thinking if Gilley and Willey had got dressed up yet, or were they playing on the floore, and wondering if Rach had got her puttys on yet, or if she was getting like you—lasy, and liked to lay around on Sunday morning. In fact, my mind was in New York. I had forgotten I was hundreds of miles away when I was suddenly startled by one of the Firemen calling out "Mr. Geer, Mr. Newton wants you down in the Engine Room." I commenced to wonder what he could want of me—if I had done any thing rong, or if he was going to give me some work to do, but my suspence was not long. I presented my self to him and he told me I was promoted to Engineers Yeoman, which in other Ships would be called Engineers Store Keeper. I get no more pay, but have scarse any thing to do. I have a nice room with a lock and key. No-one but my self is alowed in it. I serve out every thing required in the Engine room; no one can get a even [*even a*] hammer unless they come to me for it, and must return it to the Yeoman as soon as they are done with any tool. I assure you I was very much delighted, and could jump for joy, but I have had three days very hard work to clean it up and get the room to look deasant. The old Yeoman lost the position becaus he was so dirty, I think. It was as dirty, filthy [*a*] Room as I ever had to clean, but I have it looking like a pin and shall keep it so. I was not sorry to get away from the fires, as I commenced to find it very hard and hot work. My hands are very badly Calised, but they will come off now, and if I keep my place I will come home looking respectable

. . . I suppose you see very little about us in the News Papers, as I hear the powers that be will not allow any thing to be published regarding us. We had quite a sad time last evening. About 6 oclock a Boat went on Shore from one of the Gun Boats that came up yesterday. . . . They had been on Shore but a fiew moments when they were fired on by the Rebels, and all Killed or taken Prisnor except one officer and 4 seamen who were in the Boat. They pushed off and rowed for their ship, but before they had hardley got clear from the Dock the Officer was Killed and three of the Saylors wounded so bad they cannot recover. Out of all the Boats Crew only one came back

> We received orders to fire our Incindiary Shell on the town and burn it down, but several Boats came out to us from the Dock and beged us to give them time to get their familys away, and all claimed to be Union Men, but we know they all lide.
>
> — MAY 20, 1862

THE RIVER

whole, and he probably would not had it not been for the Monitors guns, as we threw a shell at them which soon sent them flying.

We received orders to fire our Incindiary Shell on the town and burn it down, but several Boats came out to us from the Dock and beged us to give them time to get their familys away, and all claimed to be Union Men, but we know they all lide. There is not a union man on shore, but the Comodore concluded that he would give them time to move, so they went at it, and all night long and this morning the Boats are passing with Furniture, Pigs, Chickens, Negros, and all other kind of property. When we will Burn the Town I hardley know. I think we will not Burn it at all, but will make the inhabitants all moove and keep them away. It looked hard to see familys compeled to pack up every thing and move from their homes at so short a notice—not half of them knowing where to go. It seamed crewel, but such is War, and the lives of our Officers and men are as valuable as their homes and Treason. Some of the people who came on board we[re] honest and owned they were for Jef Davis, but they were Old men that knew their age would be a protection to them.

The Counterbands come off to us every night but we send them back in most cases, as we have no room for them. We have one as Ships Cook. He is a likely, smart Darkey; Says his master owns 100 Slaves and is a Colonel in the Rebel armey. We are laying in front of his farm, and a most splendid one it is. They have some 8 or 10 Darks on the Galena, as they were so short handed, having so many killed and wounded.

You will not have to say in future that your Husband is a fireman on the Monitor, but that he is Engineer Yeoman. I have to keep a set of Books of the running of the Engine, and of what Stores are used.

But I commenced by telling you of Sunday morning fortune, and now what did Sunday afternoon bring? The Male, with your Lettor, and two Papers from Troy, with an account of the Fire. It was fortunate I had a room to go to to get out of sight and be alone, and I cride like a child. I could not help it. . . .

The Gun Boats and transports are coming every day. We will have quite a fleet when we make another attack on that fort. . . . I hear we are to go up to Washington for repairs as soon as we get through here. I dont think I shall ever be far away from you—probably not farther than I am at present.

The Captain has gon on Board of the Galena, and will not be back for two or three hours yet, and I want to get some money to send you, so I will have to put this Lettor one side untill he comes. It is very hard, so the boys tell me who have tride to get any money from him, unless you have a good reason for wanting it and considerable of it coming to you.

The Captain has come and I asked him for $15. He told me there was very little money in the Ship . . . and that he could not give it to me. I told him I had a family that neaded it, and I had been away three months, and left them very little, but it was no use. He told me I was not entitled to draw only the ½ pay untill the ship went out of Commission, but that he would give us all some as soon as he got a supply from Washington. If it had been Captain Worden, he would have given out the last cent if a man wanted it to send to his family. This Captain is a damd old hog, and if I ever get out of the Navy you will not catch me in it again, I can asure you. But I have learned something sence I have been here that I hope will be of some servase to me when I come home. . . .

Your Love

George

Dear Wife

Letter together with the
and Masonic print and what a treat
to hand and several days
it will last one several days
the Silk has arrived We are coaling
wrote wating for it We would have
day a job we would have
to day a flew a gale from the
morning Our Paymaster has
the that the

Four

INTERLUDE

THE JAMES RIVER OPERATIONS stalled now, just as the land campaign seemed to bog down with most of McClellan's army encamped within a dozen miles of Richmond. The action shifted to the Shenandoah Valley, where Thomas J. Jackson—now known as Stonewall—led a small army in a lightning campaign against several independent Union commands. The Richmond armies seemed to recline and watch this dramatic aside until the final clash on June 9, after which Jackson's army disappeared for a time.

Despite his new shipboard occupation as engineer yeoman,

U.S. Navy biscuit ration issued to a Union sailor on April 24, 1861, twelve days after the Civil War began. Biscuits were baked to rock-hard consistency so they could be preserved for long periods.
FROM THE COLLECTIONS OF THE MARINERS' MUSEUM.

Geer began to grow bored again during this lull. Even so, historians can be grateful that he used the free time to explain his daily activities to Martha. Occasionally, as on May 20 and 24, he wrote her two letters in one day. Beyond the *Monitor's* culinary deficiencies, the routine he described did not differ much from that on most warships of the day.

U.S. Steamer Monitor
City Point, May 20, 1862

Dear Wife

I hardly know what to do this evening to while away time. I thought I would write you a fiew lines and in that manner get read [rid] of part of the eve[n]ing, but what will I write about? I wrote so much before I am out of news. I think I did not tell you before that I have no night watch: I can go to Bed when I like, and can lay untill Six if I pleas. But I cannot sleep after foor, and am up and have a good wash and clean my Room before Breakfast.

I told you I would write you how we Live, and what we eat, so I will give you a little sketch in this. To commence, on Sunday as every other day, the Boatswains shrill Whistle is herd a[t] six, and every body must turn out and lash their Hammock up and stow them away. All hand[s] make their

way on deck, get a pail when their turn comes, and have a good wash. Most of them strip to [the] wast and wash, so you see there is not many dirty ones among us, although there is a fiew. At seven Oclock—as we on ship call it, Six Bells—the Boatswains Whistle is sounded for Grog and Breakfast, which consist[s] of a Pot of Coffee and hard crackers, such as I gave you a sample [of] on the North Carolina. But our mess is more fortunate than some: we have an Iron Sauce Pan that will hold some three or four Gallons. Our Cook takes those crackers and brakes them up, puts some fat Pork in it (of which we have plenty, as it is so fat no one can eat it), puts salt and Pepper in, and cooks it untill the crackers are soft, and that makes us what we hungry men call a good Breakfast, but what I should hardley eat if I were home.

After Breakfast, every thing is cleaned up about the Ship, which takes about one hour, and after that there is nothing to do but keep watch, which amounts to laying around deck for the saylors and laying arund the Engine room for the Firemen. I can do as I pleas, and if any thing is wanting out of the store room when I am not here a Fireman is sent to look for me.

At twelve the whistle sounds again and

Grog and Dinner is the order. I forgot: I was discribing Sunday, and will have to go back a little before I discribe dinner. I forgot to tell you of Muster, which only comes on Sunday. At 9 oclock the word is passed to get ready to muster. All hand[s] get their Bags and out comes their Sunday go to meating Cloaths. Every body must have on clean cloaths, and at 10 oclock we are all Mustered on the main Deck and the Captain takes a look at each one as our names are called, and woe to the one who is found dirty, as he will be given over to the Master at Armes, whose business it is to take him on deck, strip him naked, and take a scrubbing brush and give him a cleaning. We have not had but one case occur; I think I had rather do my own washing.

But about our Grog and Dinner. The Grog is whiskey, and they give a Gil [*gill, or one-quarter pint*] cup twice each day, and it is equal to a good stiff horn each time. For Dinner on Sunday we have Rost Beef put up in cans and preserved Potatoes. The Potatoes taste like I don't know what—any thing that has no taste at all—and the Beef is all parts of the Cow cooked to gather untill it is next to a Jelly and will drop to Pieces. It is good where there is none <u>bettor.</u>

To be Continued. . . .

U.S. Steamer Monitor
Up James River, May 24, 1862

[THIS LETTER, MARKED "LETTOR NO. 2," FOR MAY 24, IS INSERTED HERE OUT OF SEQUENCE BECAUSE IT CONTAINS THE CONTINUATION OF THE FOREGOING ONE.]

. . . I think in my last I had just finished discribing the Beef for Dinner. Wall, I will not have to discribe any Pies or Puddings, as we

INTERLUDE

are not troubled with any Desert. We have nothing to drink, or any thing to drink out of.

After dinner it is the same thing—do nothing and sleeping untill five, when Supper is Piped, and such a supper. I am shure I will get the Gout on such high living. Our Supper consists of Tea and Crackers. The Tea is made by taking, for twelve of us, about three times as much Black Tea or Grass as you would take to make a cup of Tea for you and me, and about a tea cup full of that muscovada shugar that has such a bad taste; you recollect I got some once and we could hardly use it. Wall, it is put in the mess kettle and Boiling Water put on it twenty moments before we want to drink it, and we are surved out [of] a tin Pot full and can eat as many crackers as we may wish, which for me is usuly one.

The supper is the same every night, with the addition of Butter on Tuesday and Thursday and Pickles Wednesday and Friday, but I cannot see the use of Butter quite so strong. We are none of us weak, but perhaps the Government is fearful we will get so, or it may be that they get the strong Butter to go with these Strong Crackers. Each man has his own Crockery, which consists of a Tin Pot Pan and Spoon. Geo. S. Geer is a little more aristocrattic, and has a Knife & Fork, which every body uses and I hardly know how we would get along with out them.

The mess has only two Pieces of Crockery: the Tin Pail in which we draw our soups, wash up dishes, make tea & Coffee in, and most every thing else the Pail is used for. The other is a large oval Tin Pan, and in that the meat is kept, Duff made, and so forth. On Mondays, Wednesdays, and Saturdays we have Been Soupe, or perhaps a bettor name would be to call it Bean Water. I am often tempted to strip off my shirt and make a dive and see if there really is Beens in the Bottom that gives it the flavor. I think there must be, but I seldom see them. But the Government say Beens are very Wholesom and strengthning. I am of the same opinion. . . .

On Tuesdays and Fridays we have a dish called Duff. I will give you the recpt [recipe], and you can try it. Take ½ lb. Flour to each person and wet it all untill it is a thick paste, then put in one ounce of Dride Apples to each person—cores and dirt—without cutting them up or Washing them, then put them in a Bag over night and Boil them in the morning until it is about half done through. Then cut it up with a knife so as to make it as heavy as poseable, and put a spoon full of comon Molasses on each mans piece and you have one of our crack Duffs. You must not put any yeast or any such stuf in it, or you will be shure to spoil the flavor and you will not receive half the good from it as it will be apt to work out of your stomac in the course of time, and this Duff is war[ra]nted to stay and the Apples have so much the taste of <u>Plums.</u>

To be Continued.

With the increasing heat of a Tidewater Virginia summer, *Monitor* crewmen who could swim shed their uniforms and jumped over the side, supervised by an officer with a boat's crew ready to throw a line; the officers took a boat up a nearby, more private creek.[1] His own bathing experience gave George Geer a rare opportunity to examine the artwork some of the deck hands had collected upon themselves.

". . . I wish you could see the bodys of some of these old saylors: they are regular Picture Books. [They] have India Ink pricked all over their body. One has a Snake coiled around his leg, some have splendid done pieces of Coats of Arms of states, American Flags, and most all have the Crusifiction of Christ on some part of their Body," he wrote in his letter of May 24.

Though intensely loyal to his country, Geer

On Mondays, Wednesdays, and Saturdays we have Been Soupe, or perhaps a bettor name would be to call it Bean Water. I am often tempted to strip off my shirt and make a dive and see if there really is Beens in the Bottom that gives it the flavor. I think there must be, but I seldom see them. But the Government say Beens are very Wholesom and strengthning. I am of the same opinion.

— MAY 24, 1862

never pretended that patriotism led him to join the navy. Once having signed for a three-year term, he was willing to finish out the contract (barring the occasional bout of homesickness), but he did not support the Civil War as a crusade for the abolition of slavery. Like most people of his generation and station of life, he believed that blacks were less worthy than whites. It was not the keeping of slaves that irked him about Southerners, but their intention to sever the union.

May 24, 1862
U.S. Steamer Monitor
City Point, James River

Dear Wife

About Six last evening, as we were all in Swimming, the little Tug Boat Zuave came steaming up, and as she came near us the Captain called out "I have a male for the Monitor." You may guess I was out of the water and dressed in double quick time. . . . I was not disapointed about the Lettor and Paper: they came, and Welcome they were, as they are always. I could hardly get to my room, there were so many wanted to Borrow the Mercury. . . .

You appier to have had a fit of down heartedness when you wrote me, but I can sa[y] no more than what I have already—that I am as safe as I was at home, and when you hear of our having a fight you may be shure we on the Monitor are all safe. We are laying in the same place we have been sence we came here. . . . I dont know what we will do if they do not send us Stores as we are about out of every thing and have gotten along lately by Borrowing from the other Ships, but all of us are out and the Comodore says he shall send down one of the vessels if Provisions do not come very soon.

We had another of the counterbands come on board this morning; he is very white. I wish they would send every one of them back as fast as they come. I am down on this Nigger stealing. This one I wrote you we had for a cook has gotten quite important already, and one of the saylors he had some lip to gave him a smack over the mouth, which for the presant has learned him his place. He began to think him self as good as a white man, and I must say he does know as much as some of these Saylors. . . .

Your Husband
George

Isolated now from the supply and communications center at Fort Monroe, the *Monitor* crew were becoming increasingly aggravated by the lack of action. The days must have been crawling by; Geer complained that he had not received mail for ten or twelve days (though, judging from his earlier comments to Martha, the lapse had been only about a week). Toward the end of May a box arrived from Martha. Knowing his fondness for reading, she had slipped a Waverly novel into a package of treats—milk, chocolate, eggs, and sugar.

U.S. Steamer Monitor
City Point V<u>a</u>. May 29, 62

Dear Wife

From some reason we have not received any male for 10 or 12 days, and all hands are getting very impatiant to hear from the World. No Lettors, no Papers, and what is worst of all there is a vessel ariving most every day; we hale them and ask if they have any male for the Monitor and only get no for an answer. It is so provoking. . . .

. . . I am happy to inform you that the long looked for and the anctiously expected <u>Box</u> has arived. . . . The Eggs, I am sory to say, were spoiled. . . . The Milk was OK, and Chalcolate was delicious: I did not make a drink of it; it was so good I eat it all up in two days. I gave some away, <u>but not much</u>; it was to precious. The Milk I have, and use very sparringly. The Waverly whiled away one evening for me, and is now going the rounds of the Ship.

INTERLUDE

If you can spare the money I wish you would get me the latest Harpers Magazine. There is a great deal of reading in one of them, and of a very interesting nature.

Geer was proud to detail his relations with the *Monitor*'s officers. With natural competence that had helped guide him into the commissioned grades, he also made the most of the opportunity offered by his associations. As a Mason he shared a private connection with men of recognized character and reputation, many of whom achieved positions of prominence and power. Even aboard the *Monitor* his membership in that secret brotherhood distinguished him from the unrated sailors. It was attention that could not fail to prove valuable to a competent, dedicated individual. Yet Geer had a very different take on the situation: in a crew made up in large measure of English and Irish nationals, he believed that he garnered notice in part because he was a native-born American. Like the *Monitor*'s American-born officers, Geer apparently mistrusted and disliked the immigrants who made up most of the deck crew. Isaac Newton, acting chief of the engineer department, was a Know-Nothing—a former member or advocate of the defunct American Party, which, during the previous decade, had espoused the interests of native-born citizens against the pressure from arriving boatloads of aliens. Although Geer was too young to have voted with the Know-Nothings, he probably sympathized with their xenophobic viewpoint. His disdain for foreigners emerged without ambiguity from letters such as this, written to a beloved wife whose parents had both been born across the sea.

"... I am well, and like my place of Yeoman very much. One of the Officers, the 2nd Leftenant [Acting Master Louis N. Stodder], is a Brother Mason, and he is learning me all I want to learn, and what I have wished for a chance to learn for a long time. He often sends down for me to come on Deck when he is Officer of the deck, and we have [a] good long Masonic talk. It had a bad effect in one way for me to be in such good luck (as Newton is much more frendly than he used to be): the Crew say that Newton made me yeoman because he is a Nonothing and I am an american, and that I have more privlage on Deck becaus I am a Mason. But I care very little for what they say, as there is but very fiew amongst them I would notice on Shore —as, I am Sorry to say, that amongst our Crew of 40 there is only 8 of us American born. To bad, but the Officers are all Americans, so what fiew there is of us are all ok. . . ."

Isaac Newton, U.S. Navy first engineer.
This photograph, a copy of the original,
is from the Worden album in
The Mariners' Museum archives.

At last, in the early morning of June 2, the long sojourn at City Point was interrupted with a call to raise steam and move up the river to help McClellan's army. Only two days before, the Confederate commander at Richmond, Joe Johnston, had concentrated his troops on a wing of McClellan's army south of the Chickahominy River, striking it near the settlement of Seven Pines with most of the troops he could spare. Stunned at first, the Union forces recovered and, thanks to confusion on the Confederate side, held on long enough for reinforcements to make their way across the river. The battle raged for two days, in the first of which Johnston was wounded. On June 1, McClellan had sent all the way back to Fort Monroe to ask Flag Officer Goldsborough if he could send the James River flotilla toward Richmond to distract some of the enemy's forces. A day later, Goldsborough's orders made it back up the James to the advanced fleet lying at and above City Point. The two messages had traveled about a hundred and fifty miles, while the Union fleet waited less than twenty miles from McClellan's belabored divisions.

The *Monitor*'s engines had not even begun to work hard when the suction valve of the feed pump snapped off, with the delivery valve, and jammed the force pump plunger, bending the piston and connecting rods of the air pump and the plungers of the feed and bilge pumps. Mr. Newton inspected the damage, oversaw the straightening of some of the rods, and patched things together well enough that the engine would operate, if necessary. He made no guarantee of performance, however, warning instead that any of the parts could collapse without warning. What they needed, Newton indicated, was new rods and plungers. Meanwhile, the *Monitor* lay off City Point, out of range of sharpshooters on shore. On the fourth of June, a resigned George Geer wrote the news to Martha.

"Here we are again, in our same old spot. And ever sence we have been here, day & night we have been to work repairing our Engine, and have it now so it works very well, but it is not safe and is liable to give out at any time. But I do not think we will moove from here untill the pieces we have sent to New York for arive, which will take some two or three weeks, although we may go up and atack Fort Darling again, as our Engine may stand [*it*]. And if it should Brake we could in fifteen minnets disconnect our Condenser and work High Presure, as we did coming down here from the place where we Broke down. We can work along so, but only at about half our usual speed. You must not think we could not Fight if we were disabled, as our Turret Engines are entirely separate from the Propelling Engines and we could still Fight as long as we pleased. So you see the Monitor is all OK."

In the end, McClellan fended off the attack and held his position,

> *You may well ask if it is Hott. I think Hell is an Ice house, side of this Ship.*
>
> — JUNE 4, 1862

without the navy's assistance. In part he prevailed because, with Johnston down, the Confederate army was fighting virtually without a leader. That would never happen again, for even as the firing subsided on June 1, Robert E. Lee assumed command of the scattered divisions.[2]

As McClellan's fortunes waxed, provisions for the fleet arrived—none too soon.

"That piec of Soap came in the best of time, as we are out of Soap: not one bar in the Ship," Geer told his wife. "But we will be all right now, as a Schooner came up yesterday with a load of Stores for the Fleet, and as soon as it stops Raining we shall commence to take in ours. And we wanted them bad, as we were out of every think [*sic*]."

The *Monitor*'s summer interlude on the James continued, punctuated by encounters with slaves alive and dead. When a band of runaways made it to the <u>Monitor</u> only to be turned away, Geer seemed touched by their plight. And without any battles to fight, details of food, a toothache, the weather, even the James's supply of fish filled his letters home.

U.S. Steamer Monitor
Up James River
City Point V<u>a</u> June 9 62

Dear Wife
. . . We had for Dinner this noon Rost Lamb; it was bully. The Counterbands steel them and bring [*them*] off to us some times. They bring 2 or 3 Sheep to a time, but the Officers have alwas taken them. This time they had more than they could eat, so they gave the Crew one Sheep.

INTERLUDE

I wrote to Gilbert, asking him to write to Washington to try and get me apointed Acting Engineer. If he attends to it, I think I will get it. I will pass the Examination, and the Engineers here will recommend me. The Pay of a third Eng. is about $75 pr month. . . .

I was on Deck the other day and the Body of a Negro came floating down. He had probably been shot while trying to escape. It was a sad looking sight for me, but these old Saylors only made fun over it. One was for getting his Boots; he thought it a shame to see such a good pair of Boots floating off. Another was for pulling him up to get the Eels out of him; thought by the looks he was full of them. And so the jokes went around.

About the only Fish there is in this River is Bull Heads, or Cat Fish, as they are called, and Eels. One of the Engineers, Mr. [*Albert B.*] Campbell, made an Eel Pot and set [*it*] last night. He caught some 10 or 12 lbs. of Eels.

The weather has been very Changable for the pas ten day[s]. and there has been a Cold drisling Rain for two days, so that an Over Coat does not feel bad. We have a number down with the Chills and fevor, but I keep in my room, where it is Cold, and do not go on deck only when obliged, so I do not think I will catch them. We have caught several Barels of Rain Water, and it is Cold as Ice. It is good, I tell you, to get a good cold drink; it makes me think of Home and Ice water. . . .

. . . I hope I may be able to spair enough when I get out of here to have my teath repaired, as they require it very much. I am troubled with the Tooth Ach considerable, but do not think enough of our Doctor to let him pull it.

. . . The counterbands still come to us. While I am writting you we have two men and two Woman, all of them young, not over twenty two or three, in the Engine Room, drying their Cloaths as it Rains very hard. They came from a Plantation some five miles up the River.

As soon as it stops Raining they will be put in their old Boat and be sent away with the Captains advise to go home again. . . .

One of the Engineers loaned me a Book on Engineering and one on Menseration, and I spend most of my time studying them. It gives me imployment, besides learning me something that will be usefull if I should follow Engineering.

Your loving husband
George

The heat inside the *Monitor* grew increasingly troublesome as the Virginia summer progressed. If Mr. Ericsson (who boasted of the good ventilation on his craft) did not understand the defect, George Geer and his compatriots did. Anchored now on an obscure stretch of the river below Drewry's Bluff called Devil's Reach by the pilot (and Pull and Be Damned by the sailors), the iron hull became an oven.

U.S. Steamer Monitor
James River
City Point, June 13, 1862

Dear Wife

. . . Our River Pilot came with us under the impression we were to return to Hampton Roads as soon as we had a fight, and he wants to get home very bad, and our Captain let him go and see the Flag officer this morning and he told him the Monitor would not stay here long. · She would, he thought, be sent to the Washington Navy Yard and go out of Comission, as the Government were aware she was not properly ventilated for men to live in in hot weather, and I do not think she will ever go in another action untill she has some alteration made, as the men would drop at the Guns before they fought half [*an*] hour. We took the tempriture of several parts of the ship, or rather I did, as I have charge of the Thurmomitor, and found in my Store Room, which is farthest astern, it stood at 110; in the Engine Room 127; in the Galley, where they Cook and after the Fire was out 155; on the Berth Deck where we sleep, 85. I think the hottest day I ever saw in NY was up to 102 in the Shade, so you can see what a hell we have. I spend most of my time in pleasant weather under an Awning on Deck, and sleep there these hot nights. . . .

Yours

George

By the middle of June 1862, people from the Canadian border to City Point were beginning to wonder why George McClellan did not strike a blow at Richmond. Still unsettled by the battle of Seven Pines, the Union commander made careful plans for the reduction of the Confederate capital. He hesitated to launch an assault until every company lay in place, while public opinion grew impatient. George Geer concurred. The excitement and intrigue of naval life had worn perceptibly thin for him, at least so long as he remained among the nameless ranks of enlisted men.

The *Monitor* wardroom had sunk into similar gloom. Paymaster Keeler yearned for a leave of absence after only six months in the navy. Lieutenant Jeffers applied for repairs at the Washington Navy Yard, where they all might expect to be allowed ashore, but when Goldsborough rejected that request Jeffers begged for a diffferent assignment. Acting Master Edwin V. Gager, who had been on the *Monitor* less than three months, even sent in his resignation from the service, but the Navy Department refused to accept it.

"All on board are getting tired of this life of inactivity," wrote Keeler, with admirable understatement.[3]

Dear Wife

You will see by the heading of this Lettor that we are not at City Point. We are at Pull and be Damed, a bend in the river some 15 miles above City Point. . . . [I] hear that McClellon is to make his attack on Richmond on Tuesday, but do not know how true it is. I hope he will take it soon, as we will go to Washington as soon as he does. But if he should be driven back we will lay here all summer. You will probaly know before you get this what the result is.

The . . . Galena came up to day. She played a Yankee trick. She has two Wheels to stear by—one in sight on deck and one below, out of sight. Capt Rogers had some old Cloath riged up so as to look like a man and put at the Wheel on Deck, and some more Cloaths fixed the same way on the look out to represent the Pilott. The Rebel Sharp shooters spide them and commenced to fire, and as soon as they commenced Captain Rogers answered them with some 30 or 40 Cannon and Grape Shot, which they say made them scatter pretty fast. The Old Cloaths were Riddled with bulletts. A pretty good trick.

You say that Strawburys are only 2¢ pr Basket. I am glad of it. I hope you will get fatt on them. . . .

We had a very severe Thunder storm accompanyed with Hale Stones yesterday, which cooled the air considerable, so it is quite pleasant to day. . . .

I am getting pretty well taned, as our caps have no front Piece to them, but I expected that and it will all come off again.

I wish very much you could have your Photograph taken, and send me a coppy. Even if it was one of those small ones it would be very welcom. I do long to see you or your picture so much. I am very sorry I did not think to tell you to put one of your Ambrotypes in that Box you sent. . . .

The Jacob Bell went on a Thieving Excursion on Saturday and stole a Number of fine Calves and Sheep. We got one Calf and two Sheep, but dont think they were for the Crew. The Crew could Kill them and look at them as much as they liked, but when it come to eating the Officers attended to that part. . . .

Your Loving
George

Daily, Geer and his shipmates confronted reminders of the officers' exalted status—an advantage made all the more annoying by Lieutenant Jeffers, who failed to temper his captain's position with the paternal regard that had so endeared John Worden to the crew. Aboard the *Monitor* these days, any culinary treats that came the way of the sailors and firemen were only leftovers from the wardroom.

"The Jacob Bell went on a Thieving Excursion on Saturday and stole a Number of fine Calves and Sheep. We got one Calf and two Sheep, but dont think they were for the Crew. The Crew could Kill them and look at them as much as they liked, but when it come to eating the Officers attended to that part. . . ." Geer noted ruefully.

Yet George Geer was sometimes on the receiving end of tidbits provided by the wardroom steward, Daniel Moore. Besides his skill in the galley, Moore was known for his frolics with the bottle—which seemed to be all navy stewards' principal preoccupation, if the diaries of sailors from other ships are any indication. Moore's fondness for alcohol was fed by his ready access to it: he had botched the first formal dinner aboard the *Monitor*, just before it departed the Brooklyn Navy Yard, after too rigorous a sampling of the potables he was to serve the commodore and the assembled dignitaries. A good steward usually escaped his misdeeds with light punishment, but Moore had emerged from a few hours in chains that evening to invade the officers' spirit locker for another spree that landed him back in confinement.[4]

U.S. Steamer Monitor
James River
Pull and be Damed June 18/62

Dear Wife
. . . Sence I wrote you last, our Boat went on Shore with three Officers and Five men on what they call [a] Foraging Expedition, but what I call [a] Thieving Expedition,

INTERLUDE

and Killed Five very handson Pigs, and we had Rost Pig for Dinner and have some cooking for Dinner to day. It was first Rate, and as they gave us our Rations the same we can live pretty well, but the sharpShooters are on the lookout on shore and will catch some of the Boats where they can serve them as they did the crew of the Wachusetts at City Point.

We had considerable of a time scalding and Dressing the Pigs, and it was done in good stile as we have one Butcher in our Crew. The Pigs were shot with Revolvers, and their Throat cut. One of them, after being shot several times, was inclined to show Fight, and the Saylors had to get a club and nock him in the Head.

. . . On the 17 I had been shiped 4 months. Only 4 months without seeing my Wife and little ones, and yet it may be another 4 months before I see them. But I hope and pray not. . . .

I had a tip top Supper last evening. The Cook of the Ward Room and me are good friends, and they had Veel Pot Pie for Dinner. There was considerable left, and he gave me a large Pan full. It was grand, but not equal to your make by any means. We dine on Deck under an Awning, and it is nice and cool—much bettor than eating on the Berth Deck. . . .

Your Loving Husband
George

By mid-morning on the official first day of summer, a cool breeze rippled the languid green waters of the James. In a while, George Geer would sit down again to write to Martha, making light of the danger he faced despite the monotonous duty aboard the *Monitor*. This day, he would wonder out loud about the intentions of General McClellan, and would again recount a tale of Rebel sharpshooters taking deadly aim at Union sailors—the hapless crew of the little sidewheel steamer *Jacob Bell* at Gill's (or Watkins's) Bluff. Martha probably wasn't fooled. The enforced seclusion belowdecks and sometimes extraordinary measures Geer describes being taken to deter enemy marksmen testified eloquently to the threat that stalked the riverbank.[5]

Pull and be Damed James River
U.S.S. Monitor ~~Ap~~ *June 21 1862*

Dear Wife

. . . Oh, how tedious this is. It is as bad as States Prison, as far as the confinement is consirned. The Crew, as I have told you before, is not such as I have a taste to associate with, and it makes it very loansom for me.

The Jacob Bell had a very bad time coming up yesterday. When some three miles below here she was fired in to from a high bank by 4 pieces of Field Artilery and some 1000 or 1500 sharp Shooters. The Bells Guns were so exposed the men could not work them without being picked off by the Sharp Shooters, so they had to keep out of sight and run past as fast as they could. The steamer was badly riddled and the Pilott wunded, but no body killed. She went down last night and the Port Royal accompanyed her as far as where she was attacked. The Captain of the Bell had the shoulder torn off his Coat by a Rifle Ball;

rather closter than I should like one to come to me.

We have not herd one word of news sence I recvd your last Mercury, which I believe was of the 7th. We know McClellan has not made an attack on Richmond yet, as we should hear it, as we are only 12 miles from there. Why he does not make an attack we cannot contrive. . . .

George.

Other sorts of disaster also were omnipresent. At midnight on June 22 the watch rang the alarm for a fire inside the ship. With the *Monitor's* execrable ventilation, it was nothing short of miraculous that a galley fire failed to overcome those who tried to fight it in the confined space below the turret.

The vagaries of mid-nineteenth-century medicine picked up where sharpshooters and shipboard fires left off. Acting Assistant Surgeon Daniel C. Logue, whose ministrations to the crew thus far had consisted mostly of stimulants, treated Geer for a wrenched knee by plying him with purgatives. Perhaps the doctor reasoned that if he completely drained his patient of fluids, the swelling in Geer's knee would have to subside.

U.S. Steamer Monitor
City Point June 23 1862

Dear Wife

. . . It is now most two weeks sence I have herd from you, and I am most crazy to hear if you are all well. . . .

You see this Lettor is dated at the old place. We came down from pull and be Damed to day to gather with all the rest of the Gun Boats, leveing nothing up the River above this, and I can assure you we were very glad to get away from such a god forsaken place. Nothing but Swamps on both sides of the River, with exelant places for these cursed Sharp Shooters to pick us off every time we came on Deck. . . . On the way down the Captain made us all keep below Deck, ready if the Rebels fired on us to return it, but they did not try it.

About 12 oclock last night we were all turned out of our

Hammocks by the watch with the word that the Ship was on Fire. We soon found the Deck timbers around the Galleysmoke Stack was on fire. We have Hose to reach from the Steam Pump in the Engine Room to any part of the Ship. They were at once lade, and a stream put on the Fire that soon put it out. I suppose nothing will be said about it, as people would smile at the idea of an Iron Ship getting on Fire, but then they do not know we have wood inside. But there would be very little chance for a fire to get under much head way, as there is always some 10 or 12 on watch at a time. In all Men of War there is an arangement to Dround the Powder Magasine and Shell Room. Here we can by simply turning a Cock, full them with Water in five moments, so there would be no chance of us Blowing up.

I am still under the

doctors care with my Nee. It is swolen quite large, but is not painfull unless I give it a sudden bend. I think if I was home and had some Arnaca Linament I would cure it in one day. The only thing the Doctor is doing to me is to fisic me, and he is doing that thorough. I feel as though there was nothing in me—not even a gut left—but it will get well of its self soon.

Our Engine worked very bad coming down to day. She is all out of order, and we will have to go to some Navy Yard soon to repair. How I wish it was to NY, but no, I don't think this Boat will ever see NY again. It will undoubtedly go to Washington.

How is the weather in NY? It is quite cool and comfortable here. In fact, we are having so much cold and so fiew hot days that it astonishes the natives.

. . . I am at a loss to know why we were brot down and the River abandoned above here. There must be some reason for it, but cannot surmise what it is, but time will tell.

The water in the River is getting very warm, and it always has a bad taste to it and is very muddy, so we are not much bettor than we were in Hampton Roads. . . .

Your husband
George

Under the orders of the secretary of the navy, but with little personal confidence, Louis Goldsborough had forwarded an underwater explosive device up the James, where it was to be used to the best advantage. Commander Rodgers, the acting flag officer of the impromptu fleet at City Point, devised a plan to employ it in the destruction of a key railroad bridge over Swift Creek, which ran into the Appomattox River below Petersburg. Though Geer did not know it, this plan lay behind the wholesale Union navy withdrawal from the upper James, for Rodgers planned a diversionary attack on City Point to allow safe passage for the Appomattox expedition, which included the *Monitor*. Once the gunboats had reached as far upstream as they could, boatloads of saboteurs were to row farther on with the submarine *Alligator* and blow the 250-foot-long bridge into the river.

At the behest of George McClellan, the navy on the James devoted itself to this daring little project for most of a week. At long last, McClellan intended to move against Richmond, which he feared would be heavily fortified from south of Petersburg. Gustavus Fox thought the attack would be a valuable accomplishment if it were properly coordinated. Indeed, in a few days there would be plenty of activity in McClellan's direction, but it would not particularly come of the young general's initiative.[6]

US Military

Harrison Bon[?]ry

Dear Wife

this morning and thought I would try
be anxious to hear from
good letter as I have written
you sence I wrote
other two make
to commence last
I wrote you
— on the sick list
Sunday was my
made so sick
gave me Medicin
try and get the
I throw them up considerably
to day I feel much
trouble is a diar[?]
produced on
Yellow as su[?]

this morning and know[?]ing
what they have
be taken care of
last that you had I dont
know what he
no doubt but Elethorp
make him
de wonders in a
be as likely to
him as any
but dont think I
him for I do not
here the male comes
day so our Lettors
the weather has
the last few
as I suppose are

writing for the
went up the
found a house
one of the
had room for
them all but
very hard to see
what you had
morning you had
but I want

give
commen[?]
day the

Five

THE RETREAT

WHILE THE NAVY ORGANIZED for its excursion up the Appomattox, McClellan moved the first troops in what he supposed would be the last battle of his Richmond campaign. After breakfast on the morning of June 25, 1862, eighty-three days after his departure from Fort Monroe, he ordered Joseph Hooker's division forward along the Williamsburg Road from the intersection at Seven Pines. Hooker ran into heavy resistance, and the brigade on his right all but fell apart an hour or two into the fighting. By late morning the firing had died down, but McClellan himself came up and renewed the contest that afternoon. The sound of the battle carried easily to City Point, where sailors speculated on the significance of the affair by its volume.

"Yesterday we could hear very heavy and rapid fireing most of the day," Geer wrote to Martha on June 26. "I suppose many poor fellow[s] bit the dust. . . ."

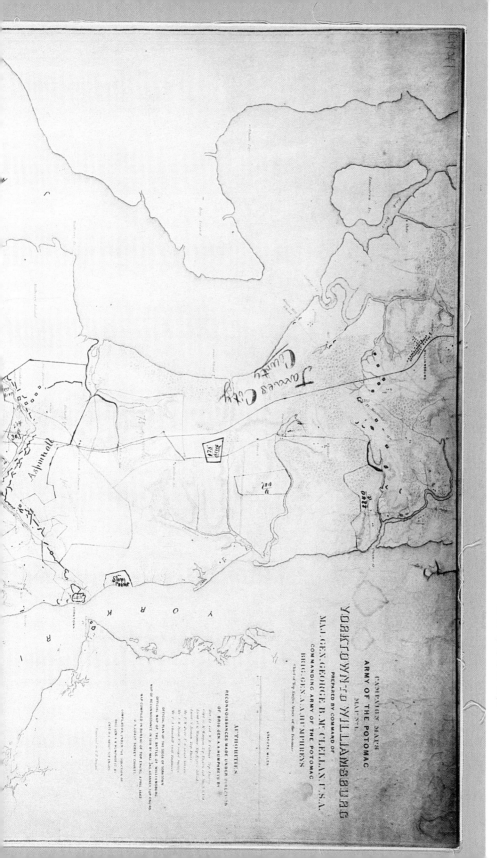

*Campaign map for
General George McClellan's
Army of the Potomac,
showing key landmarks
of the area between the
lower James and York rivers.*
FROM THE COLLECTIONS OF
THE MARINERS' MUSEUM.

> *Things look here as though we were going to make another dash on Fort Darling [Drewry's Bluff]. Yesterday Comodore Goldsborrough came up and brot a Submarine Mashine to blow the Sunken obstructions out of the River. With what vessels have arived here the last few days, we have a large fleet of Vessels. I suppose we will make a moove very soon, as I think they are Fighting up there every day.*
>
> — JUNE 26, 1862

General Lee had planned his own attack for the next day on the other end of the opposing lines, and had moved most of his troops in that direction for his first offensive as commander of the Army of Northern Virginia. Now, rather than upset those plans, he chose in characteristically daring fashion to let the two Confederate divisions in that vicinity dig in and hold off an assault of eight divisions of their adversaries.

Through the first day of fighting, there was little change in the opposing positions. The next day, the *Monitor* sailors, nearly two dozen miles from the clash, apparently could not hear gunfire, though it achieved greater pitch in a shorter span. This was Lee's assault near Mechanicsville, north and east of Richmond. From the beginning, the action had not gone as Lee hoped. It began late and cost him four times the casualties of his entrenched opponents. But the assault did accomplish one important change: it marked the day he took the initiative from George McClellan, and for the next twelve weeks he would not relinquish it.

Dear Wife

Your three Lettors . . . are, as usual, full of kindness and love. If ever a man had a good wife, I have one. You write complainingly or Jelously of the comfort and pleasure other wifes seam to enjoy with their Husbands when you see them walking to gather of a Sunday. But you should feel very proud to think your Husband is not a Coward at home, but is fighting for a country for his Wife and Children. And at the same time be thankfull that I am not in some of these old Wooden tubs. . . .

. . . If I could only draw what money I have coming to me and send to you [I] know it would enable you to help Uncle and pay what you are in debt to Rachel. I must have some $35 due me, but do not think I will be able to get it untill we go to Washington, and that will not be untill Richmond is taken.

Things look here as though we were going to make another dash on Fort Darling [*Drewry's Bluff*]. Yesterday Comodore Goldsborrough came up and brot a Submarine Mashine to blow the Sunken obstructions out of the River. With what vessels have arived here the last fiew days, we have a large fleet of Vessels. I suppose we will make a moove very soon, as I think they are Fighting up there every day—I mean the Armeys. Yesterday we could hear very heavy and rapid fireing most of the day. I suppose many poor fellow[s] bit the dust. . . .

Your
<u>George</u>

Casualties on June 25 and 26 were the heaviest of the campaign so far—yet they would count as mere skirmishes compared to the rest of that week. After noon on June 27 most of Lee's army came down on a single Union corps commanded by Major General Fitz John Porter, who had ensconced his troops on high ground just north of the Chickahominy River, which separated him from the rest of McClellan's army. Gathering in front of a milldam owned by Dr. William Gaines,

THE RETREAT

Southern divisions outnumbering Porter two to one hammered him for nearly eight hours before he escaped across the river. Some eighty thousand of the blue and gray took part in the battle of Gaines's Mill, and by nightfall more than twelve thousand of them had been shot, nearly 2,400 having been killed outright.[1]

As Geer anticipated, the *Monitor* men had embarked on their own little campaign up the Appomattox. At dusk of June 26, as the firing subsided at Mechanicsville, the *Monitor* steamed up from City Point behind a flock of steamboats and two gunboats, with others following. As the flotilla crossed the bar into the Appomattox the gunboats sent shells screaming into the countryside, hoping to distract the enemy from the real target of the expedition—the dynamiting of the railroad bridge. While most of the ships anchored just below the mouth of Swift Creek, two continued up the Appomattox toward Petersburg. The *Monitor's* Lieutenant Greene had been selected to lead one of the boats towing the submarine *Alligator.* Midnight had passed when Greene returned to the ironclad. Below Petersburg rebel sharpshooters had opened on one of the tow vessels, the *Port Royal,* and the other, the *Maratanza,* had run aground. Under wither-

Lieutenant Samuel Dana Greene.
From the Collections of The Mariners' Museum.

ing fire, the daring experiment had been abandoned.

All the next day, while the battle raged near Gaines's Mill, the flotilla remained just downstream of Swift Creek. During the second night tugs labored to drag the *Maratanza* into navigable water, but no sooner had they succeeded than the little *Island Belle* ran into the shallows and stuck there. The other boats threw lines to her, but around noon on June 28 news of McClellan's defeat and subsequent retreat reached the ears of

The Monitor Chronicles

"The gun-boats 'Galena' and 'Mahaska' shelling the rebels at Harrison's Landing, July 1, 1862." Engraving from Harper's Weekly, *July 26, 1862.*
From the Collections of The Mariners' Museum.

the officers of most vessels. That sealed the doom of the *Island Belle,* which felt the torch as soon as her crew and battery had been removed. Then the ships all turned downstream. At City Point the helms all swung left, up the James, and by nightfall the would-be raiding vessels had reconvened in Devil's Reach. Eventually word of the Union debacle reached the sailors: Union troops were on their way to the left bank of the river.[2]

Completely cut off now from his supply base on the Pamunkey River to the north, McClellan started his army south, toward the James. Jubilant Confederates struck his retreating columns at Savage's Station, on June 29, and again at Glendale on June 30. Late that night the fleeing Federals reached a long, low slope called Malvern Hill, less than two miles from a big loop in the James. Here the fugitives rallied, ringing the hill with field guns. Commander Rodgers came up with the *Galena* and the *Mahaska* to lend the persuasion of their nine-inch Dahlgrens and hundred-pounder rifles. The *Monitor* returned to City Point, unable to lift her muzzles enough to be of any use.[3]

The Retreat

113

The next morning, while artillerymen on both sides of Malvern Hill rolled their pieces into line for a massive duel, an ailing yeoman on the *Monitor* scribbled a long letter home.

U.S. Steamer Monitor
James River
July 1 1862 City Point

Dear Wife

. . . I have been quite Sick for the past week—not with my knee, as that is well, but with a complainte half of the Ships company have been down with; what to call it, I dont know. It first affected my Bowels and water. I have no apetite, sick to my Stomac, and very week, but I am over the wors of it am [and] am getting bettor and stronger every day. I eat a fiew Crackers that came out of the Ward room and a very good cup of Tea for my Breakfast, the first I have eat in three days, so you see I am improving and no doubt will soon be attending to my duties again. . . .

. . . I got a lettor from Gilbert. He has sent a petition to the Secretary of the Navy to have me examined for an Engineer and sent it to Mr. [Abram] Olin, the member of Congress from Troy, who I am very well acquainted with. Gilberts says if Olin attends to it, and he has no doubt he will, that I may look for an order any time for my examination. . . .

. . . Dont worry your self about sending me the Harpers if you are short. You need not send it untill you can spare the money. How sorry I am, and how provoking, to think I have money enough coming to me to relieve all your presant wants and cannot get it. To day is the end of the Quarter, and I have about $5.00 coming to me for Grog, which, according to the rules of all Government ships, is paid every Quarter, but I hear we will not get it as there is no money in the Ship.

What there is, some $200, the Captain wants for his own gutts. He is a damd old Gluttonous Hogg, and I hope the curse of Hell will rest on him. You may think it strong language, but it is as I feel, as well as all the ships company.

. . . Sence I wrote you last we have been sturring around considerable, but . . . have accomplished very little. We went up the Apiamatic River towards Petersburg and shelled the bank on both sides. It was in the night, and the intention was, after we got up the river as far as we could, to send a boat expedition up the River some 5 miles to burn a Rail Road Bridge, but we found that the Sharp Shooters were to thick. We could not accomplish our object. One of our Gun Boats, a small one, the Island Bell, formaly a tug around NY, got a ground and we were obliged to set her on Fire, as the sharp Shooters were so thick we could not get her off. A tug came up while we were up the Apamatic with orders for us to go up the James River. We went up some 15 miles and came down Yesterday. There is a large Armey here, and it was to protect them we went up the River, but we did not find them untill we came back here again. There was a sharp Engagement las evening between them and the Enemy. What Troops they are, or where the[y] came from I cannot find out, but I am fearfull they are part of McClellans Armey, retreating. If so, wo be to this Cuntry, as it will lengthon out this War at least six months. . . .

Your Husband
<u>George</u>

That afternoon, as George Geer pondered the fate of McClellan's forces, the guns opened on Malvern Hill. The two gunboats launched their huge shells. When the barrage stopped, the Confederate infantry swept forward much as it had at Gaines's Mill. But this day the men in gray advanced in an uncoordinated rush; the blue lines held their position, mowing down their opponents as they came. The outcome was slaughter. Lee lost nearly twice the three thousand casualties McClellan suffered, and—in contrast to their previous meeting—the blue divisions kept control of the field. Yet despite this sudden, significant victory, the next morning the Yankee army continued its retreat, striking through a driving rainstorm for Harrison's Landing, where the navy could protect it.

The next day, July 3, found the Confederate army arriving on the fringes of the Federal army. Scanning McClellan's position,

Engraved miniature of the battle of Malvern Hill, ca. 1863.
From the Collections of
The Mariners' Museum.

Lee found it too intimidating for an attack. In the security of Harrison's Landing McClellan was also neutralized, but a deciding factor in Lee's decision not to attack seemed to be the gaping mouths of the guns aboard the U.S. Navy's vessels. On July 4 Lee wrote President Davis that he did not "wish to expose the men to the destructive missiles of his gunboats."

One of those gunboats, of course, was the *Monitor*. On that day, the original of her ironclad class lay with three wooden gunboats at the mouth of Herring Creek. There, or near there, she would remain for almost two months.[4]

On July 4, the *Monitor* took a cruise upriver with the six-gun side-wheel steamer *Maratanza* as far as Turkey Point, a hairpin bend of the river near Malvern Hill. As the pair rounded the bend they were surprised by an armed Confederate tugboat, the *Teaser*. As gunfire spurted toward the little flotilla, the *Maratanza* ended the tug's career in three shots. Her crew broke for shore; while they disappeared into the rolling Virginia countryside their crippled steamer drifted into Union hands. Aboard, the Yankees found an observation balloon and equipment for use in electrically detonated underwater mines. They unfolded diagrams of mines suspended in the upper James, as well as a map showing their locations. And they rifled through a packet of papers that included orders directing Lieutenant Hunter Davidson, formerly of the *Virginia*, to take over command of the submarine batteries on the James. One of those to flee the *Teaser* a few minutes before, Davidson had left behind his sidearms and some personal effects. The Federals amused themselves by reading a letter his wife had addressed to "My Splendid Hunter."[5]

On the *Monitor's* deck, Paymaster Keeler witnessed the capture and, while his ship took no active part in it, he pondered the possibility of realizing some prize money from the small triumph. Officers saw far more generous rewards than did enlisted men (Keeler later heard tell that they would have shared a million dollars had they sunk the old *Virginia*). The chance for remuneration ought to have inspired comment from the sailors—yet Geer did not even mention the affair. He may not have heard about it, and he certainly saw nothing of it, for Geer had fallen victim to hepatitis.

"I am still under the Doctor care, but worse than I was when I wrote you last," he wrote to Martha on July 5. "This time it is my Liver is out of order, caused by drinking River Water. What water passes me is the color of Blood, and I am as yellow you would think I had the jaunders, and I am so weak I can scarce stand alone. But I think I have seen the worst, and shall commence to get bettor at once."

In the 1860s, the only treatment for hepatitis was rest and time. Surgeon Logue ordered both for Geer, who spent a solid, miserable week in sick bay, on the floor of the berth deck. Logue also applied the same treatment he had relied upon to reduce the swelling in Geer's knee—a hefty dose of purgatives. Geer recovered despite such ministrations, and credited the surgeon with having healed him.

"I am as Yellow as safron, have no apetite," he wrote on July 8, "and have not tasted any food for five days. . . . The Doctor says it is bettor for me not to eat, but that as soon as my apetite returns—which it will do as soon as my Liver acts—that I will eat like [a] horse. I find him a much bettor Doctor than I had put him down for. I have no doubt I will come around all right in a fiew days under his care."

U.S. Steamer Monitor
James River
Harrisons Barr July 8 1862

Dear Wife

. . . Wall, to commence, I have been very sick sence I wrote you last, and shall probably be on the sick list for some time. . . .

I suppose you have seen an account in the papers of our doings, and that we are covering McClellons army. Sence I wrote you last we have been most of the time imployed running up and down the River watching the Rebels and driving them off. I think the Rebels would have driven McClellans Army in the River had not the Gun Boats been here to protect them.

You say you should feel easy if you knew the Monitor was in Order. Wall, you can feel easy, as our masheenery is know [now] in good order and works like a Clock. . . .

There is a very large fleet of Schooners and Steamboats here; it reminds me of NY, there is so many from there (I mean Steamboats). They are most of them used for Hospitals, and I hear the wounded are treated to every thing poseable to get them: plenty of Ice Water, Ice Lemonade, and as good Food as the Market affords. . . .

I commenced this Lettor this morning, but as we received orders to get up

Anchor and go up the River I had to stop writting for the want of a place to write. We went up the River some 15 miles and found a house filled with wounded Solgers. One of the other boats took 7 Boat loads of them. We did not take any, as she had room for them all, but we could see them all put on board, and it looked very hard to see the poor fellows and think what they have suffered, but they will be taken care of now. . . .

I have not herd yet from Gilberts aplication to have me appointed an Engineer. . . . If I do not hear from it in about a week I shall write Gilbert and he says he will try another plan that he thinks will work. . . . I am out of Postage Stamps. Can you send me a fiew?

We have not signed our accounts for the first of July. I have most $5.00 coming to me for Grog, which they must pay, but I hear there is no way to get money but to send our Pay Master down to Hampton Roads for some, and that he is going tomorrow. . . .

Your George

> We went up the River some 15 miles and found a house filled with wounded Solgers. One of the other boats took 7 Boat loads of them. We did not take any, as she had room for them all, but we could see them all put on board, and it looked very hard to see the poor fellows and think what they have suffered, but they will be taken care of now.
>
> — JULY 8, 1862

The day after Geer finished his July 8 letter, while the *Monitor* lay anchored, an artist attached to McClellan's headquarters came aboard to capture the only photographic images the world would ever see of the curious little ship. He snapped Lieutenant Jeffers before the turret, alone, and then arranged the other officers in different poses in that same location. Next he pulled his apparatus back on the deck so the off-duty watch could stand for him a couple of times; later he caught some of the officers lounging near the edge of the ship, with Mr. Stimers's reinforced pilothouse peeking around the turret. More than half the crew appear in the resulting prints, including the contraband kitchen helper, but not George Geer: he lay below, too sick to climb the ladder. In a few days, however, on July 12, he would be well enough to pen a long letter to Martha, giving a careful account of happenings aboard the ironclad and offering his forthright opinions on the conduct of the Union army as well as *Monitor*'s official affairs.

LEFT TO RIGHT: *Robinson W. Hands, third assistant engineer;*
Acting Master Louis N. Stodder; Albert B. Campbell, second
assistant engineer; and Acting Volunteer Lieutenant William Flye.

Officers of the USS Monitor, July 9, 1862 (James River).
FRONT ROW, LEFT TO RIGHT: *Robinson W. Hands,*
Albert B. Campbell, and Edwin V. Gager, acting master.
MIDDLE ROW, LEFT TO RIGHT: *Louis N. Stodder,*
William F. Keeler, acting assistant paymaster; William Flye,
and ship's surgeon Daniel C. Logue.
BACK ROW, LEFT TO RIGHT: *George Frederickson, acting*
master's mate; Mark T. Sunstrom, third assistant engineer;
Lieutenant Samuel Dana Greene, executive officer;
Lieutenant L. Howard Newman, executive officer
aboard USS Galena; and Isaac Newton.

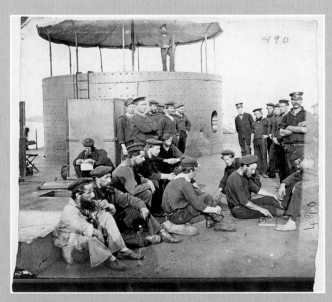

Most of the Monitor's crew on deck, July 9, 1862.
George Geer is missing from this photograph.

Scenes from the deck of the Monitor.
FROM THE COLLECTIONS OF
THE MARINERS' MUSEUM.

Harrisons Landing V*a* July 12, 1862

Dear Wife

I received your welcom Lettor and the Mercury, and the next day a Ledger, both Papers containing pieces [of] Soap, which I can assure you was very welcom. . . . The account of McClellans retreat was the only full account we had had amongst the Crew, and I read it aloud to a very interested audiance. They are all very much attached to the Mercury, and look for it as much as I do, and share in my disapointment when it does not arive.

The Soap I gave one piece away. You may think that strange, but I will tell you why. I gave it to the Wardroom Cook. He has been very kind to me, and I have often received a nice mouthfull from him, which he would hide away for me while cooking, and sence I have been sick he would give me part of his own meals when I would eat it. And as his Hands and Face were very sore from using the Salt Water Soap I thought I was under obligation enough to give him on[e] Piece.

I was sorry to hear you

had the Face ache and blews on July 4. but I suppose you have gotten over them by this time. . . . If you knew how much I thought of you on the 4 you would not wounder at your expecting me, as my thoughts went to you although I did not in person. You could not see me, perhaps, but I was there.

As regards my sickness, was it not for the Doctor giving me Medicine and keeping me on a light diet I should not know I was sick, I feel so well. The yellow color has not gon off of my Eyes and skin yet, but in a fiew days nothing . . . will be left of it. . . .

We have a new Comodore here. It is Wilkes—the one that took Mason & Slidell. He is a smart man, so they say, and we can expect to do something now. I am very glad we have got clear of Old Golsborrow. . . .

We are laying right in front of McClellans head Quarters, where we have been since the 6, and I hope we will lay here some time, or as long as it is so hot, as it heats the Ship up so it is imposeable to live in her when we are running. It Rained yesterday and the day before, so it is quite cool yet, but the way the Sun comes out this morning it will be hott enough before night.

. . . Our Paymaster has gone to Hampton Roads. . . . Our mess sent down by him for 2 bbl. [*barrels*] Potatoes and one of Onions. If he gets them, we will be able to have good Scouse for Breakfast as long as they last. It will cost us about 1.<u>oo</u> Each man. . . .

We had quite a good joke happen. A suttler has come up here to Suttle for the Navy, and he came here to get permission to call every day and sell them men what they wanted, and in Consideration of the privlage he was to send the officers 2 bbl. of Bottled Porter. Our boat was sent to his Schooner and brot back the 2 bbl. One of them was opened, and out of 7 Dozen Bottles eleven whole ones were found. The rest were thrown overboard. The other Barrel was opened and found to contain White Crushed Shugar, so they kept the Shugar and called the thing square, as the Shugar is worth about $30 or 40, the price it is sold for down here.

I hardley know what to think about the Armey. Some say that it will be reinforced and moove on Richmond again in two or three weeks . . . and others say that there will be no moovement until cold weather sets in. I hope that the moovement will be made at once, before the Enemy has time to make their defences any stronger. . . .

Your George

Throughout his stint aboard the ironclad Geer took pains to assure his wife that the *Monitor* offered the safest service in the war. Yet, as the summer of 1862 sweltered on, his superiors had begun to doubt both the ironclad's effectiveness and invulnerability. Reports circulated that the Confederates had almost finished their own new armored ship, the *Richmond*—built in the image of the *Virginia* but on a smaller scale, for the close combat of river warfare—and rumors floating down the James suggested that she could sink anything afloat, including the *Monitor*. Noting that the *Monitor* seemed "exceedingly overrated in prowess," Admiral Goldsborough asked if he could have one of the new Union ironclads then nearing completion.

That observation was one of Goldsborough's last as commander of the flotilla on the James. Commodore Charles Wilkes arrived in the second week of July to assume command, carrying orders to report directly to the Navy Department. Stripped of the most active part of his squadron, Goldsborough felt as though he had been rebuked, and soon asked to be relieved of his duties altogether.

Wilkes's rise differed sharply from that of his predecessor. He had achieved prominence eight months before when he stopped a British ship and removed from it the Confederate diplomats James Mason and John Slidell. The resulting international furor brought Wilkes popular support in the North and a promotion to commodore. (Unfortunately, the administration had to release his prisoners to avoid war with England.) The *Monitor*'s sailors also approved of their new leader. "We have a new Comodore here," Geer wrote Martha. "It is Wilkes—the one that took Mason & Slidell. He is a smart man, so they say, and we can expect to do something now. I am very glad we have got clear of Old Golsborrow. . . ."

Yet this difficult, ambitious officer would achieve no more with the flotilla than Goldsborough had. To the increasing disgust of Washington officials—and the Northern public—neither the navy nor the army appeared inclined to do anything along the James for the rest of that summer.

Meanwhile, in early July, Paymaster Keeler journeyed to Hampton Roads to collect supplies. With him he carried special grocery orders from the different dining messes, for if sailors wanted palatable food they had to pay for it out of their own pockets. They usually pooled their resources and bought groceries through an officer, but

I was sorry to hear you had the Face ache and blues on July 4. but I suppose you have gotten over them by this time. . . . If you knew how much I thought of you on the 4 you would not wounder at your expecting me, as my thoughts went to you although I did not in person. You could not see me, perhaps, but I was there.

when their ships lay near a sizable anchorage they could sometimes avail themselves of the services of a sutler. The army attracted hundreds of these traveling merchants, who offered various delicacies, tobacco, or special camp equipment, with the occasional bottle of whiskey sold under the plank that served as their countertops. For all of this they charged extortionary prices. To ensure that penniless soldiers could be lured into a purchase, the sutler was usually willing to accept a signed receipt, which he would present to the next paymaster who visited the regiment. The sutler's bill had to be resolved before the soldier took his first dollar.

Sutlers were much less frequent visitors to navy vessels, but early in the *Monitor's* sojourn at Harrison's Landing one appeared, offering an ill-disguised bribe to Lieutenant Jeffers in the form of two large casks of bottled beer. As it turned out, there was more in the transaction than Jeffers had planned. "We had quite a good joke happen," Geer reported gleefully in his July 12 letter. "A sutler has come up here to Suttle for the Navy, and he came here to get permission to call every day and sell them men what they wanted, and in Consideration of the privlage he was to send the officers 2 bbl. of Bottled Porter. Our boat was sent to his Schooner and brot back the 2 bbl. One of them was opened, and out of 7 Dozen Bottles eleven whole ones were found. The rest were thrown overboard. The other Barrel was opened and found to contain White Crushed Shugar, so they kept the Shugar and called the thing square, as the Shugar is worth about $30 or 40, the price it is sold for down here."

When Commodore Wilkes inspected his new command on July 12 he found the *Monitor* "defective," as he had been warned. Whether the defect lay in the apparent delicacy of her engine or in the unbearable heat generated by her boilers, he did not say in any list he may have compiled. She ought to be sent to Washington for overhaul, he seemed to suggest, but for the moment he preferred to keep her on hand in case the army needed some riverside artillery support.[6]

As Geer would tell his wife, the *Monitor* crew learned more about the war they were fighting from the newspapers she sent him than they could from the seat of the conflict, and that summer those newspapers ran thick with information about the national government's first attempt to draft troops. Part of General McClellan's justification for remaining idle at Harrison's Landing lay in his constant demands for more troops, for he believed himself outnumbered despite his actual superiority in manpower. In July, in an effort to raise an overwhelming force to suppress the rebellion, Congress revised existing legislation that required each of the states to provide its share of militia against a national levy of 300,000 men. If enough volunteers did not come forward for nine months of active service, each state would be required to fill its quota by selecting from its enrolled militia—that is, from prepared lists of male citizens between the ages of twenty-one and forty-five. It was the closest

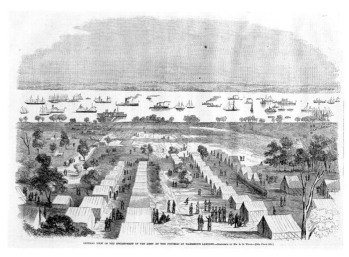

The encampment of the Army of the Potomac at Harrison's Landing, Virginia.
Harper's Weekly, *August 23, 1862.*
From the Collections of The Mariners' Museum.

the United States had ever come to a national draft, and it excited widespread fear and resentment. It would take a more comprehensive draft law eight months later to exert much influence on the number of men in uniform,[7] but on July 15 Geer hinted to Martha that even the militia draft may have prompted some men to think of alternative service.

"It seams all the assertions I can make of my safety here do not seam to assure you," he complained. "You should think how much bettor I am than as though I was in the Army at $13 pr. month, and perhaps if I was home I mint [might] be drafted and have to go. So I think, taking every thing in consideration, I am in the best place I could be. You would think so if you could hear these Soldiers wish they were only on the Monitor in place of in the Army. . . ."

U.S. Steamer Monitor
James River V<u>a</u>
Harrisons Landing July 15 62

Dear Wife

Sence I wrote you on Saturday I have received a Lettor on Sunday, a Lettor [with] Medicin and a Pass Book on Monday, and a Harpers on Tuesday. I am sorry you sent me the Medicin and Harpers: the Harpers because it cost money you need your self and the Medicine because it is of no use. You must recollect to take Homeopathy Medicine it is necessary not to drink Coffee, and to go without Coffee here would be to go without Breakfast, and while I am on the Dr. list I must take his medicine as he gives each dose him self and sees you take it down. So it would be useless to take this Medicine you have sent. But I will take care of it, and if it should return on me I will Doctor my self. At presant I am as well as ever and am done taking Medicine, but the Doctor will not let me go to work yet. He says he wants me good and Strong so I will not be back on the list again, so you see I have it very easy as regards work, but very hard trying to kill time.

That Blank Book is exactly the thing I wanted; Harpers is very interesting. I was up reading untill 12 oclock, and this morning have most finnished it. . . .

I had this morning the first good Breakfast I have had sence I have been in the Navy. Our Paymaster came back yesterday and brot the long looked for Potatoes and Onions. I have not found out yet if he brot any money or not. . . .

We are still laying at our Ancorage and there is no news. This place was the home of Wm. Henry Harrison, President of the U.S., and the house occupied by the Army was the one in which he was Born.

The inclosed card I wish you would give to Jonney and ask him to go down to the place and ask Mr. Baker [*apparently, a source for items wanted by* Monitor *cook Daniel Moore*] if he has received any Lettor from the name on the Back. Moore is the Cook who was so kind to me. Tell him to ask Baker if he has received any Lettors (Moore has written him 7 or 8) and if he has if he is going to send him those things he sent for. If not, he will give me the money and let me send it to you, and have you send the things. . . .

You appear by all your Lettors to be very down Hearted and unhappy. I expect when I come home I will find you as poor as a Crow with your anxiety and starving your self to be saving. It seams all the assertions I can make of my safety here do not seam to assure you. You should think how much bettor I am than as though I was in the Army at $13 pr. month, and perhaps if I was home I mint [*might*] be drafted and have to go. So I think, taking every thing in consideration, I am in the best place I could be. You would think so if you could hear these Soldiers wish they were only on the Monitor in place of in the Army. . . .

George

Soldiers visiting the *Monitor* that July might well have wished themselves elsewhere. They had concluded a long, exhausting campaign with a bloody week of battle in which their only victorious field had been abandoned; now they lay in a camp beset by clouds of mosquitoes and mysterious fevers, watching their comrades sicken and die while generals and politicians puzzled over what to do next. Assailed by those same insects and similar ailments, the men of the *Monitor* would remain on the James as long as the army did.

U S Steamer Monitor
Hampton Roads Apr 13 1862

I received your kind but
I notice you it was
I know you was getting
like find hang you

on board and
the Merrimac
in to see her
and Sewels Point
would all day to see
col come so we had
disapointed yesterday a
Trooks were mooved from
Norfolk and this morni
a very large Explosion
nothing could be seen
after it so we had
at once to Norfolk
our disapointment
leveing that the
Norfolk at 5 oclo
so we started
of the vesels
back we

he wants to distingu
with her as Capt Worden
he has a chance
praid Worden
praying for him to
my Love to Rach and

Six

THE LANDING

THE LAST TWO WEEKS OF JULY passed quietly for the *Monitor*. George Geer's health was improving, while his worries about his family's precarious finances grew, fed by resentment.

There was reason for Geer and other *Monitor* sailors to be resentful. Paymaster Keeler had returned from Hampton Roads with plenty of money for the *Monitor*'s cash box, but Lieutenant Jeffers, tightfisted as ever, refused to grant sailors their wages beyond the few dollars allowed for grog. Geer concluded bitterly that beyond the half-pay sent automatically to Martha, he would never be able to wring any money from Jeffers. The hardship Jeffers's behavior posed for Martha Geer outraged her husband, for the navy no longer had the excuse that he might desert before he had earned his money. Geer also may have known that officers had no pay withheld, so their families could exist in relative comfort—knowledge that must have rankled all the more. Whereas Keeler could deposit two hundred dollars into his wife's account,[1] Geer could not draw even fifteen dollars so his wife could supplement her meager household groceries. On July 18 he would close a letter to Martha with bitter words:

"I see by the Herald they are trying to get up an excitement by holding mass meetings, but I think that has very little inducement to get men to inlist. The best thing is some guarantee that their Famalys will be taken care of properly. What a swindle the Navy is to a man with a family: he can only leve ½ pay, and the ballance he must wate untill his time is out for unless the Captain he is with is disposed to let him have it, as it all lays with him. . . ."

Geer wanted the means to augment the paltry income that did come his way, and soon he found it—in the elevated status, and opportunity, afforded by his regular mail from home. His newspapers, for instance, circulated widely among the crew; even the officers looked forward to the New York papers for accounts of their military situation that were more reliable than the tales relayed by combatants.[2] With Martha as his reliable source, he also could offer his shipmates certain coveted small items; if Martha could avoid express costs by tucking the merchandise inside a newspaper, the couple would profit that much more. Always cautious, Geer decided to begin his enterprise with a single item that he could use himself if no customer materialized. This initiative, and critical observations on the behavior of his fellow sailors, made up much of the rest of his letter of July 18.

Monitor
James River
Harrisons Barr July 18 1862

Dear Wife
Your Lettor of the 13 came to hand yesterday. . . . You see by the enclosed money that I have at last recvd my Grog money, $4.80,

and send you $2, and will send you two more the next time I write. One Dollar was in debt for my share of the Onions; I paid with the 80 c an Postage stamps. . . .

I enclose you a piece of Silk Thread. It is called Sadlers Silk. I want you to enquire what you can buy it for by the Pound, and if you can spare the money I wish you would purchase a ¼ of a Pound and send it, part to a time, in the Mercury. And count the Skeins and let me know how many there is in ¼ lb. I want it to make up a Flannel Shirt with, and as most every body has drawn the Flannel and there is no Silk in the Ship I think I could sell it and make something on it if I got it at once. If I could not sell it at once a ¼ lb. would be no more than I would use my self. . . .

We are laying some foor miles farther up the River than we were when I wrote you last. We are on McClellans left Flank, so if the Enemy attempt to out flank him we can give them some of our 11 in. Grape. There is not much Juce in the Grape, but if they hit a secesh Regiment I have no doubt they will draw the Claret. . . .

There has been considerable Gambling here sence the men got their money, and some would not have any thing coming to them if they were at sea all their lives. They will draw the Flannel and Satinett, and make up nice Cloathing, and then put it up for Raffle and them [sic] Gamble the money away. I can never see the point, and always keep clear of their Games. In fact, I keep by my self so much that the boys boys [sic] dont recon me one of the Crew, but a kind of half Passenger. The English and Irish portions of the crew are out with each other, and have several times come very near having a general fight, and have had several small fights. I wish they would have a big fight and eat each other up, so we could get clear of some of them and get some deasant men here—if there is any in the navy, which I begin to doubt. . . .

THE LANDING

◄●►

> *We are laying some foor miles farther up the River than we were when I wrote you last. We are on McClellans left Flank, so if the Enemy attempt to out flank him we can give them some of our 11 in. Grape. There is not much Juce in the Grape, but if they hit a secesh Regiment I have no doubt they will draw the Claret.*
>
> — JULY 18, 1862

I have come to the conclusion that we will have to stay in this River untill Richmond is taken, or untill one of the new Monitors are completed to take our place.

I see by the Herald they are trying to get up an excitement by holding mass meetings, but I think that has very little inducement to get men to inlist. The best thing is some guarantee that their Famalys will be taken care of properly. What a swindle the Navy is to a man with a family: he can only leve ½ pay, and the ballance he must wate untill his time is out for unless the Captain he is with is disposed to let him have it, as it all lays with him. . . .

Your Loving Husband

<u>George</u>

When Geer next wrote, the release of a crewman whose enlistment had expired had exacerbated his sense of entrapment.

"One of our crew who only shiped for one Year got his discharge yesterday and is now on his way home," Geer informed his wife. "He is a marid [married] man and lives in Road Island. Oh, how I envid him his discharge, but he was as glad to get it as I could poseably be. He thinks the Government will never get him again. He says he will stay in the merchant servace, where he can see his family once in a while and have plenty of good vittles to eat, and if he happens to get with mean and overbairing Officers he can leve them."

At home Martha's situation had gone from bad to worse. So pinched had the household budget become that Martha had taken a part-time job laundering clothing for a friend. "Taking in washing" was at the lower limit of respectable poverty in 1862, and Geer—already suffering the embarrassment of having to borrow from relatives to support his family—reacted first with anger, then understanding.

"You write me you have turned Washer woman. I was provoked—I may say angry—when I read it, but the more I think of it the more I

Some days sence, one very hot day, I went on deck and as usual squat down on the deck on the Shady side of the Tower. While I had been down below, the tide had turned the vessel around and brot the side where the sun had been poring all day, around in the shade. I, unfortunately, had forgotten a rip in the seet of my Pants, and I can assure you I got up quicker than I set down, and with a very stinging sensation in my sett down. I think I shall keep my Pants in good order, in future.

— JULY 20, 1862

think perhaps it is for the best. At any rate, it shows I have a Wife that is willing to help get along. . . ."

Geer was tireless in his efforts to get ahead. He continued to work the mails for a promotion, undiscouraged by apparent administrative inaction and exploiting his political connections, which were unusual for a common sailor. Not only was he acquainted with his congressman, Abram Olin, but also with Olin's Democratic opponent in the 1860 and 1862 elections. A letter to Martha toward the end of July began thus:

Harrisons Barr Va
July 23 1862

Dear Wife
. . . Gilbert . . . says he has herd nothing from Washington yet, but that Congress would adjourn on the 17the and as soon as Olin got home he would see him and find what he has done with the Petition of mine, and if he has not presented it to the Secretary of the Navy Gilbert says he will send it to somebody in Washington and pay them to attend to the matter and push it. . . .

Olin and other Democrats promised to do well in 1862, partly because the war they partially supported seemed to be bogging down. George McClellan, the favorite of the Democratic party, blamed his recent setbacks on the government's failure to give him all the troops he had asked for, and now, from his base at Harrison's Landing, he was asking for more troops to conduct another campaign against Richmond. As Geer deduced in his July 23 letter, McClellan wanted to ship troops across the James to attack Petersburg from the south, cutting Richmond off from the rest of the Confederacy and enabling the Federals to simply wait for the Confederate capital to be starved into surrender. His superiors did not like this plan, although nearly two years later they approved it for Ulysses Grant, who would ultimately finish off Lee's army on that line.[3] In the summer of 1862 some people still hoped for a more timely conclusion to the war, however, and as Geer's detailed letter of July 23 indicates, he was one of them.

U.S. Steamer Monitor James River
We had two secret boat expeditions this week. They had their Oars muffled and you could not hear them ten ft. from the Vessel. They made an examination of the River on the South Side and found the Water very

deep clost in Shore, and some very fine places to land. I think Burnside will land on that side and take Petersburgh and so on, up to Richmond, while McClellan goes on the North side or drives the Enemy back where the[y] have driven him from. By that means the Gun Boats would go up at the same time, and with Burnside in the rear and the Gun Boats in front I think we would make very short work of Fort Darling. And if the Armey had posession of the Banks, which it would, it would prevent their exploding any Tanks of Powder in the River, or any of their sharp Shooter picking off our men, and if we once get up to Richmond with the Gun Boats it is a gon Goos [gone goose].

You ask if I think they will ever take Richmond. My answer is, most certainly, yess. It may be two or three months before they do take it, but I am satisfide that all the energys of the Government will be to take Richmond. I will not say this Monitor will be in it, as I think and hear that some of the other Vessels that are building will be done in two Months. If so, I suppose they will take our place and let us go somewhere for repairs. I hope they will hurry them up. I wish you would ask Wm. Henry to go over to Green Point some Sunday and see if he can find out how they are getting along with them, and how soon any of them will be done. If you see any thing in the Papers about them, cut them out and send me. . . .

Your loving Husband,
Geo. S. Geer

Clearly, Geer had gotten wind of a rumor that Ambrose Burnside's North Carolina army would come to McClellan's assistance. Troops from Burnside's command were unloading at Newport News, and in a day or so Burnside himself would be up to Harrison's Landing for a chat with his old friend. With him would come the new general in chief of the army, Henry Halleck, who would argue against McClellan's desire to keep the Army of the Potomac on the line of the James River.[4] When Halleck returned to Washington, however, he left McClellan with the impression that the army would be allowed to make one more attempt—and the navy would stay as long as the army did.

Reading Geer's letter now, it is clear that the sailors on the *Monitor* had their own views about ways out of the James River doldrums. If Richmond could be taken, the war might come to an abrupt end and, theoretically, everyone could go home except a couple of divisions of occupation troops. Short of that, if the ship were laid up for lengthy repairs at some navy yard—presumably the one at Washington—there was a fair chance the crew would get a leave of absence with money in their pockets.

As it would turn out, neither option would come to pass. With the Confederates reportedly wrapping up construction of their new ironclad *Richmond* a few miles upstream, the U.S. Navy was not about to let the *Monitor* leave the James until another ship of the same shotproof class arrived to take its place. Each day seemed to bring a different estimate of how long that would take, but few held out hope for an early deliverance. The *New Ironsides*, an ironclad with a battery that could throw nearly a ton of metal with each broadside (and the vessel for which Flag Officer Goldsborough had been lobbying), lay a month away from commissioning at the Philadelphia Navy Yard. Other replicas of the *Monitor* were rumored to be in the ways at Green Point, where the prototype had been built, but their status remained a mystery to the James River fleet.

Meanwhile, the Geers' enterprise in the notions market paid off immediately, if not handsomely, prompting Geer to consider expanding his line of offerings. Unlike those who followed the sea for a living, he was married to his supplier and so could rely on her. His friend Moore, the wardroom steward, one of the gullible boarders mentioned in Geer's letter of July 27, didn't have such luck. Geer's brother-in-law had visited Moore's Water Street correspondent, who always answered Moore's inquiries with the claim that the goods had been duly posted.

My Dear Wife

Your two Lettors came to hand: one yesterday morning and the one with the Silk in this morning. The silk I sold before I had time to finish reading your Lettor. I sold it for one Dollar, and I think if I had not sold it so soon I could have got more. I want you to send me some more as soon as you can. I think it will come as quick and safe in a Paper as to pay 9¢ Postage, only it would not do to send it all in one Paper. I wish you would enquire the price of Red, White, and Blue Silk: the same kind. I shall want to send for some of both. I think A number of the Crew have sent for Silk, but none of them get it. They send to their Boarding Masters, or men they have boarded with when in NY, and they get Lettors from them stating they have sent it, but it never comes. They are so green they cannot see through the game, but blame the Express and Post Office. But I know that where they do not get it is becaus their swindling Boarding House Keepers put the money in their pocket and write poor Jack they have sent it. So you see, I think I can sell several ounces of it. . . .

Around this time some of *Monitor's* men (though not Geer) showed symptoms of scurvy, due to their vitamin C–deficient diet. Officers on the ironclad also had little fresh fruit or vegetables, but in other ways they ate rather high on the hog—often literally. So rich a diet had its disadvantages. Lieutenant Jeffers was subject to attacks of gout, worsening his surly disposition. When he was in pain, men of all ranks suffered.[5] In this respect Geer may have been the luckiest man on the ship: his duties kept him occupied in the storeroom, and since he had already concluded that he would have

Scale model (⅙₆") of the Confederate ironclad ram gunboat CSS Richmond, *made by William E. Geohegan.*
From the Collections of The Mariners' Museum.

no luck getting money from Jeffers, the only time he had to risk the commander's presence was Sunday muster.

Another kind of drama also was unfolding aboard the *Monitor.* A mechanic and Union sympathizer who had worked on the *Richmond* at Norfolk had taken his recollections of the new ship's dimensions, armor, and armament across Hampton Roads to the U.S. Navy shops at Fort Monroe, where his old boss from antebellum days was master machinist for the North Atlantic Blockading Squadron. Together the pair worked out rough drawings of the ship, which was a shorter version of the *Virginia* with four guns instead of ten. Within days the senior officers on the James had all seen those plans.[6] It wasn't long before the purloined specifications, or a creative version of them, had reached the berth deck. Geer confidently (and erroneously) told Martha, "You write about that new Merrimack. We have the pleasure of having an acurate Drawing of her: she only mounts 5 [*sic*] Guns, and so much of her hull is out of the Water that we calculate it will take us about half hour to send her to the Bottom. She is nothing near as form[id]able as the Merrimack, and the Rebels have no intention of sending her down to attack us, but they will keep

You say you wish the Paymaster would hurry up and give me some money. You may as well give up expecting any, as he has plenty of money, and the Captain will not let us have one cent. He is sick with the Rumattic Gout, and I hope to God it will use him up or at least cause him to give up the command and go home, and let some deasant man take his place. . . . But I cannot hope for any such luck unless we should get to some Navy Yard, which we will as soon as one of the New Monitors are finished and come here and releve us. Do find out how they are getting allong with them if you can, and let me know. . . .

— JULY 27, 1862

her above Fort Darling to dispute the passage of the River if we take the Fort. If she does not worey you any more than she does me, you will not worey much."

News traveled as quickly among the land forces as it did in the flotilla. An unofficial visitor to the *Monitor* from a nearby infantry regiment carried a piece of speculation on future military movements that hinted he may have known something about the generals' conference at McClellan's headquarters a couple of nights before, after which it appeared the army would gather reinforcements and prepare for another assault on Richmond.

For the crewmen of the crippled *Monitor*, July 30 provided a taste of

THE LANDING

their halcyon days at Hampton Roads, when the entire fleet had looked to them for protection against the enemy's most formidable warship. At mid-morning lookouts announced a plume of black smoke billowing above the treetops upriver, and the call brought everyone's eyes to the horizon. At Sewell's Point that cry had usually heralded the approach of the *Virginia,* and now everyone assumed this would be the *Richmond,* newly completed and coming down to do battle. Boat crews splashed homeward with errant officers and men, signal flags went fluttering up the halyards of masted vessels, and Commodore Wilkes scurried about the flotilla in a tug, barking orders through a trumpet. Every ship within sight wallowed up behind the *Monitor,* which lay waiting to make the first challenge. While coal clattered into the fireboxes and the boilers began to whistle,[7] George Geer once again spent his spare moments composing a short letter home.

U.S. Steamer Monitor
James River July 29 [30] 1862

Dear Wife

I . . . am required to give something out of the Store room every fiew moments, and it is to hott to stay in there long at a time, so I must make my Lettor Short. I think I wrote you in my last that my Friend Moore had got a Lettor from that man Jonny went to see. He says he sent the things, but I think he is a lire, and that he has sent nothing but is going to keep Moores money and fool him, and Moore thinks the same so he is going to give me the money to send you and have you send him what things he wants.

I wish after you get your money on the first you would get one of the Packages of Brown Winsdor Soap and send me. You, I think, had bettor put one cake in a paper. Send me the Price and I will send you the money. Of corse I will try to make something on it and send you.

The Monitor *Chronicles*

I shall send you all I can make on any thing. I shall want you to send me ½ oz. of Each Dark Blue, White, and Red Sewing Silk, the same size as the Black.

We are under Full head of Steam, ready to start any moment, as there is a Smoke up the River and we are fearfull it may be the Merrimack. . . .

Yours

George

Nearly a score of gunboats waited that morning, afternoon, and evening, but all that came down the river were more rumors. Paymaster Keeler, who could light a candle in the relative privacy of his tiny stateroom, waited until after the ships returned to their anchorage at about 9:00 P.M. before detailing the anxious day to his own wife. Keeler supposed that the scare would end their frolics and foraging ashore.[8] Geer hadn't been off the ship since it left New York, and since he had mostly avoided the purloined food officers had brought back from their adventures, he didn't have much to lose from any new strictures imposed by the *Richmond* alarm. If he lost sleep, it was due to a toothache, which had only one remedy in those days. Martha had the same problem; apart, they suffered together.

That summer Geer also had to think about the coming winter, for the mountains of coal consumed by the fleets threatened to drive up the price for city residents, and speculators were already maneuvering for a fast buck. "I am sorry there is a prospect of Coal going up," he would write home on July 31. "I wish I could send you the money to buy a Ton with."

Geer was also looking with hope to the *Monitor*'s deteriorating propulsion system—if it failed or needed overhauling, he might get at least temporary relief from service.

"I think it cannot be more than two Months longer, as our Engine and Boiler are getting sadly in want of repair and our Blower Engines will have to be replaced with new ones, as they are almost worn out," he noted. "You see, they have been run most 6 mos. without stopping. All the time they are stoped is about 5 moments in 24 Hours to Oil them."

But the hottest topic of conversation on the berth deck of any United States warship late in the summer of 1862 was the decision of the adjourning Congress to eliminate the twice-daily grog ration in the Federal naval service. With the temperance movement taking firm hold in the country,

Anti-Southern, anti-liquor cartoon engraving from Harper's Weekly, *March 15, 1862.*
From the Collections of
The Mariners' Museum.

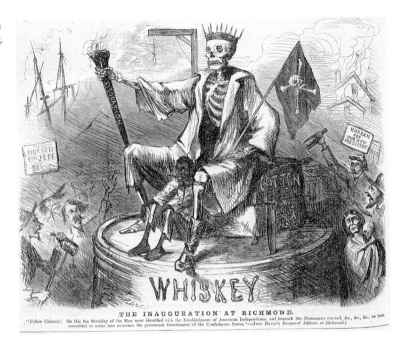

THE INAUGURATION AT RICHMOND.
"Fellow Citizens! On this the Birthday of the Man most identified with the Establishment of American Independence, and beneath the Monument erected, &c., &c., &c., we have assembled to usher into existence the permanent Government of the Confederate States."—(Jeff Davis's *Inaugural Address at Richmond.*)

many states had passed prohibition laws in the 1850s; now the same spirit against spirits took aim at the one arm of the government that regularly distributed liquor. As soon as the orders reached them, ship captains from the Gulf of Mexico to the Strait of Gibraltar began reading the decree from their quarterdecks at Sunday muster—an announcement some of the older salts greeted with an air of high tragedy. Not Geer.

"I suppose you see by the Papers that Congress has passed a Law which takes effect the 1st of September, stopping the Grog in the Navy and giving them 5¢ pr. day in place of it," he wrote. "Of corse the men take it to Heart very much, and swore they will never come in the

The Monitor Chronicles

Navy again, and that it will be imposeable to get good Saylors, but my opinion is we will have bettor men and plenty of them. I started my Grog this month, and probaly have drank it some ten or twelve times, so you see it has cost me, or I will not get my 120 for this month, but I shall drink it no more. I drank it becaus the Water is so poor. . . . I believe that Liquor in the Navy has made many [a] Drinkard, and I am glad Congress has put a stop to it."

U.S. Steamer Monitor James River
Harrisons Bar July 31 1862

Dear Wife

Although I wrote you yesterday, still I was obliged to stop so short in order to get it in yesterdays mail that I did not feel as though I had written you any Lettor, especialy after receiving your lettor last evening. It was one of the sort I like to get. It makes me sleep bettor when I can go to my Hammock with a knolidge that you are all well—or all except you. . . . I am with you, for night before last I was up half the night with one of my Teath, and burned my mouth half off raw with Alcahall, but it does not ache now and I hope will not untill I can get on Shore, when I will have it taken out with several other troublesom ones.

I was writing you yesterday about the new Merrimack, or as the Rebels call her the Richmond. Wall, we have learned that she is done, and all ready to come down. Yesterday the Galena saw a Smoke up the River that looked as though it came from a Steamer. We were ordered to be ready for action, and were in five moments ready for a Fight. When the Smoke was first seen only the Galena and Monitor was at the Bar. The other vessels were some three miles below, but in less than one hour I could count Eleven Vessels mounting over 50 Guns, and most of them the very heaviest kind, and all the vessels are Steamers, so there will be no more Sailing Ships like the Cumberland for them to catch aground and sink. I think the Rebels are not such fools as to send their one Ship to contend with such a fleet as this, and Old Comodore Wilks does not mean the Monitor shall have all the fight, as he is clost to us with his Ship, the Wachusetts, and all cleared ready for action. That is something like a Comodore, and diferant from old Golesborrow, who was always trying to get away as far as poseable when there was a prospect of a fight.

Your two Papers came all right, including the Soap and the Candy. Tell Willey Papa sends a kiss for the Candy, and when he comes home he will buy him a lot of Candy and take him up to the Central Park. Poor little fellow; I wish his Papa could tell him when he would be home, and I have no doubt his Mother would like to know very well. What do you think? I think it cannot be more than two Months longer, as our Engine and Boiler are getting sadly in want of repair and our Blower Engines will have to be replaced with new ones, as they are almost worn out. You see, they have been run most 6 mos. without stopping. All the time they are stoped is about 5 moments in 24 Hours to Oil them. . . .

I suppose you see by the Papers that Congress has passed a Law which takes effect the 1st of September, stopping the Grog in the Navy and giving them 5¢ pr. day in place of it. Of corse the men take it to Heart very much, and swore they will never come in the Navy again, and that it will be imposeable to get good Saylors, but my opinion is we will have bettor men and plenty of them. I started my Grog this month, and probaly have drank it some ten or twelve times, so you see it has cost me, or I will not get my 120 for this month, but I shall drink it no more. I drank it becaus the Water is so poor. . . . I believe that Liquor in the Navy has made many [a] Drinkard, and I am glad Congress has put a stop to it.

I am sorry there is a prospect of Coal going up. I wish I could send you the money to buy a Ton with. I . . . am glad that money was acceptable and in the right time. I only regret I have no more to send you. . . .

I hear that Engineers and Firemen are getting very large pay. One of the Firemen on a chartered tug told me he was getting $50 pr. month and the best of Board. I wish I was free now, although I do not regret what I have learned, or that I was on the Monitor.

Why dont you have that tooth out, or is it a front one? We will both of us be toothless before we are very old. . . .

Geo. S. Geer

The evening of July 31, after a Union observation balloon had made its regular reconnaissance, Confederates on the south side of the James wheeled seven dozen guns into position to bear on the sleeping camp at Harrison's Landing and the ships that lay before it. Just before 1:00 A.M. all those guns opened at once, their shells arching into the naval vessels and over them, rousing surprised soldiers and raising a cacophony of shouted commands and screams. Almost immediately, the gunboats responded. The sidewheeler *Cimarron* bore the brunt of the fight, rattling off ninety-two rounds from its two big pivots and three port-side howitzers. Army batteries soon spun around to advantageous ground, but most of their fire sailed over the heads of the Southern artillerists, who inflicted dozens of casualties in the army camps but suffered only three by return fire. The *Monitor* lay within sight of these midnight pyrotechnics, but never fired a gun. Comfortable beneath the only mosquito bar on the ship, Paymaster Keeler slept through the entire incident.

Down on the berth deck, George Geer may have done the same.[9] Geer's attention was turning more toward his sideline enterprise, which was turning a profit. Neither had he abandoned his campaign for promotion, which required that he not only satisfy his immediate superiors but persistently appeal to his political acquaintances. The ship's officers may also have shared Geer's disenchantment with the summer's rising tide of abolition fervor. Like many conservatives in the army and navy, he had agreed to fight only to save the Union.

By early August clouds of flies and mosquitoes boiled out of the Chickahominy swamps to attack the invaders. It offered no comfort to reflect that the enemy suffered the same torment.

"I thought I had seen Mosquetoes and Flies that were a nuisance in NY, but I give in to Virginia," Geer wrote in early August. "There is no use fighting. You may as well keep still and let them have their fill, because one will only tire him self out and have at last to give in to them. The way I do is not to turn in untill about 12 Oclock, or untill I think they have got their fill out of those who have to turn in early."

Dear Wife

Your Lettor with the Silk came to hand all right, except that the Onvelope was so full it had torn open, but I counted the Skeins and there was 42, so I suppose none were lost. But I think it would be safer to send only part at a time, and send them in a News Paper. . . . I have not seen a NY Dailey for so long I hardly know what is going on in the World. I want you to send me a Dispatch once, in place of the Mercury, as some of the Boys have subscribed for the Mercury and I can borrow theirs, and I am getting down on the Mercury. They are too much Abolition to suit me.

> Oh, if you only knew my feelings when I read one of your Lettors with the discription of the doings of those Youngsters, you would pitty me. I am most crazy to see them. I can see that Gilley is mothers Boy and Willey is Papas.
>
> —AUGUST 3, 1862

The silk was much finer than the last you sent, but it is what I want, and believe it is all sold although it is not delivered, nor will it be untill I see the money. But I will get the money so as to send in my next Lettor. I wrote you in my last about sending some colard [colored] Silk. I see you have sent me one skein of each; they are exactly what I want. If you can send me ½ oz. of each, do so as soon as you are disposed. I have some other things to send for, but I think I will wate till you send what I have already ordered. Be shure and get the same size and Color of that Silk as the Sample you have sent.

Oh, if you only knew my fealings when I read one of your Lettors with the discription of the doings of those Youngsters, you would pitty me. I am most crazy to see them. I can see that Gilley is mothers Boy and Willey is Papas. . . .

I . . . received a Lettor from Gilbert on Thursday. He sa[ys] Olin has got home; he went and saw him. Olin told him he presented my Petition to Mr. Wells, the Secretary of the Na[v]y, and to Mr. Fox, his assistant, and they told him they were not making any promotions in the Engineers Department at present, but should as soon as the new Monitors were ready, and that my aplication should be attended to. Mr. Olin told Mr. Wells that any[thing] they done for me he should consider a personal favor to him. Gilbert says he is going to see several men who are personally acquainted with Mr. Wells to get them to write to him in my behalf. Gilbert says for me to keep up my spirets, as there is no doubt I will get promoted before Fall. . . . I am going to ask Mr. Newton for a recomendation. He can do no more than refuse me, and I think I can get it in spite of him.

. . . I hope you will not forget to mention what you have to pay for those Buttons, as they are for one of the Crew. You would laugh to hear these poor Saylors reconing how many more tots of Grog they will get before the new Law comes in to operation. . . . Some of them will go crazy if they cannot get Liquor. . . . We had two new men come on Friday to fill up our Crew as two men have been paid off, their time being out. They came direct from the North Carolina, and they say a Crew was drafted for one of the New Monitors, but I think it must have been the Crew for the New Iron Sides. Can you hear anything about how they are getting along with the new Boats?

. . . Your Affectionate Husband

George S. Geer

For several days General Halleck had been considering whether to give McClellan the promised second chance to reduce Richmond, and by August 1 he had evidently grown so anxious about McClellan's demands for reinforcements that he had determined to order the Army of the Potomac back to northern Virginia. Halleck gave preliminary orders for the evacuation, directing McClellan to remove the sick from Harrison's Landing, but not until the evening of August 3 did he inform Little Mac of his intention to abandon the line of the James. Halleck's telegram arrived at midnight; McClellan appealed in vain. Sick and wounded Union soldiers began boarding the steamers the next day.

Before reading Halleck's decision to withdraw, McClellan had sent a large contingent of mixed troops over the river to take control of Coggin's Point, where most of the artillery bombardment had come from two mornings before. He had also sent two infantry divisions and one of cavalry toward Malvern Hill in preparation for his anticipated offensive. Even after Halleck's order arrived, McClellan continued moving against Malvern Hill on the excuse that the Confederates were rumored to have abandoned their capital. The rumor proved false, as the young general must have suspected, but even then McClellan kept the news from his troops—and, on Halleck's orders, from his officers as well. Commodore Wilkes, however, who had been collaborating with McClellan on operations upstream, got the full story of both Halleck's orders. Wilkes composed a long telegram of protest to Gideon Welles, but the secretary of the navy could not have dissuaded Halleck under any circumstances, and his late-night effort went unheeded.[10]

Dear Wife

. . . We have information which I think there is no doubt of. In fact, it came from the Chief Engineer of the Navy that we would leve for Washington as soon as one of the New Monitors comes here to relieve us, which we hear will be in three or foor weeks.

We are having sturring times at presant amongst the Fleet. They are kept busy running up and down the river and Shelling the Rebels where ever they show them selves. Day be fore yesterday the Advance Pickets of the Army were as far up as Malvins [Malvern] Hill, which they found occupide and fortifide by the Rebels. Yesterday our Gunboats went up and helped the Army to drive them out, and took some Six or Seven Hundred Prisnors, but the Monitor takes no part in any of them. She will not moove from here untill something turns up worth Fighting. Our Guns are to heavy and Aminition cost to much to be firring at every thing along shore that looks like a Rebel.

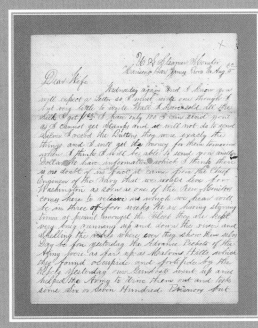

There has been five large Steamers come down to day from City Point loaded with Union Prisnors. You should have herd them Chear for the Monitor. They are a hard looking set, as they are dressed every way and shape, but when they come to get back in their own Regiments and get properly Cloathed they will be the right kind of fighting men. One of them will be worth 4 Drafted men. . . .

. . . Dont you think you could put ~~Willey~~ Gilley up in several News Papers and send him to me? I will use him well and send him back as soon as I play with the little Frog, and hug and kiss him. You must be shure and do him up nice, and direct it plain or it mint *[might]* go to the Dead ~~Baby~~ Lettor office in Washington. . . .

Your Husband
Geo. S. Geer

Some of the reinforcements McClellan had planned for early in his campaign had been withheld to protect Washington and had remained all spring and summer north of the Rappahannock River. Those troops and others from the spring's Shenandoah Valley campaign had since been organized as a separate entity, now called the Army of Virginia, under the command of Major General John Pope. In early August Pope's aggressiveness matched his boastfulness and General Halleck directed Ambrose Burnside's North Carolina divisions to Pope's front rather than to McClellan's. At about the same time on the Confederate side, Stonewall Jackson's divisions moved north to deal with Pope—a move that stripped Richmond of half its defenders. Several days passed before McClellan detected that exodus and during the night of August 6, to the astonishment of the enemy, he abandoned his advanced position at Malvern Hill and drew back to his lair at Harrison's Landing. At the moment when Robert E. Lee most expected and feared another offensive against the capital from that direction, McClellan squandered the fruits of the first step toward one, thereby tipping his hand.[11]

While McClellan procrastinated Halleck fumed. Yet a week after he had ordered the army commander to evacuate Harrison's Landing it remained a secret to most of those on the spot. Thanks to a late summer heat wave, soldiers and sailors alike appreciated a few days of inactivity. For some, it was an opportunity to liberate extra provisions from Virginia farmers. For George Geer it was a chance to concentrate on his thriving shipboard commerce.

U.S. Steamer Monitor
James River, Aug 10 62

Dear Wife
Your two Lettors [arrived], one on Wednesday and the other on Saturday evening. The Silk is all right except that there is only 16 Skeins of Blue and 21 of White & Red. How comes that? Did you take any out, or did they get the best of you where you bought it? You told me you would have to pay the same for it as for the Black, which was 5/-/6 [five bits, six cents] or 68¢, so you must have paid $1.02 for the ounce and [one] half. I sold it as soon as I opened it for $2.25, and I have 2/- on it and am to keep the Silk untill I get the $2.00. So you see, I made well off of it and hope to send you the money in my next Lettor. . . .

I want you to send me, after you send the Soap, 3 Locks and three sets of Buts (Brass) *[presumably a reference to butt hinges]*. They are for small Boxes the size of an ordinary Candle Box. I dont want Pad Locks, but regular locks with Screws for the Buts and Locks. You ask Wm. Henry, and he will tell you what to get and where you can get *[them]* cheapest. Be shure and send me the Price, as you did not tell me what the Rings cost and I have not sold them, although I have had a chance once to sell them for 4/- and perhaps may not have another such chance. . . .

Sence I wrote you last we have had Green Corn in great plenty. We send a Boat on Shore and get from one to two hundred Ears out of a Sesesh Corn Field every morning, and yesterday morning the Officers shot a Calf, for them selves, of corse: we get none of it. But as we get fresh Beef from the Government twice each week I am very well satisfide. I have eat Corn three times pr. day every day we have had it; in fact, I have not eaten any thing else. I think we will have plenty of vegitables while they last, as there is plenty of them planted around here. . . .

It is awful hot. The swet roles off of me, and I can hardly keep from Wetting this paper, although I have a Towell under my hand. We worked untill 10 oclock last night taking in Coal, as it is to hott to work in the day. We have had to give up sleeping on the berth Deck, and all hand*[s]*, Officers as well, have to sleep out on the open deck. I have been sleeping so for one week, and have caught no cold, so I think I will get along.

Dont . . . send any thing I cannot sell. I wish you would send me ~~an extra~~ Times, with as much of that Lemon Shugar as you think it would do to send, for I feel as though I would give any thing for a Drink that was palatable. You will only have to get a fiew cents worth. You can get it when you are out after the Locks. Get the Locks with two keys, if you can. If the Locks and Hinges cost more than 4/- pr. set dont buy them, as I could make nothing on them.

. . . You say Jonny will get a substitute in case he is drafted. I think he will find it very dificult to do, as they will be in demand and will be apt to command a very high price—probaly more than he can pay. The bounty is so large I should advise him to volunteer if he thought there was any prospect of his being drafted. But he has been there once, and I suppose he does not require any advise. . . .

George

On August 9 Stonewall Jackson thrashed part of Pope's Army of Virginia at Cedar Mountain, a good sixty miles northwest of Richmond, alerting the Federals that Lee had probably detached a substantial portion of his army. On that news McClellan reported on August 12 that there were apparently no more than 36,000 Confederates southeast of Richmond. With more than twice as many men, McClellan felt a bit more confident than he had during the Seven Days, and he asked Halleck for permission to take advantage of the enemy's weakness. Accustomed now to McClellan's delays, Halleck refused. In so doing he lost what would have been an exceptional opportunity had someone else commanded the Army of the Potomac, but thirty-six days later McClellan would demonstrate that even with odds of two to one he could not be counted upon for a complete victory.[12]

The continuing evacuation of the sick and the departure of some troops and artillery on the night of August 11 helped lift the veil of the impending departure. Sailing down to Fort Monroe on another errand, Paymaster Keeler deduced that something was afoot and correctly speculated that McClellan's army was going to join Pope on the Rappahannock. Confined to the *Monitor*, George Geer reported no such observations. Instead, he dwelt often upon the imminent implementation of the militia draft.

"... Things must look very serious for some of these young men who have talked fight and stade at home," he observed to Martha on August 13. "They may, some of them, have a chance to try their pluck when drafting commences, and I am glad they are going to draft, as I think it will end the War very shortly. I dont suppose they will draft any of my Brothers, as they are all over thirty, but I think they will have to draft those over before they get all they want."

To one used to associating with men of modest means (whose alternatives to conscription would have been few) the impending draft might indeed have seemed like a genuine threat. In fact, the 1862 militia draft affected far fewer young men than Geer predicted.

One rumor did filter through the crew —a rumor that Lieutenant Jeffers planned to take advantage of a loophole to supply the ship with alcohol despite Congress's prohibition.

"Our Captain is going to do something he thinks is smart," Geer noted. "The new law about Liquor says no liquor shall be brot on any Government Vessel after the 1st of

This six-inch, half-pint flask, made by the Baltimore Glass Works (Baltimore, Maryland), probably dates from the Civil War era, when such flasks were much in vogue as liquor bottles. The raised decoration on this one was designed to appeal to sailors or seafarers. FROM THE COLLECTIONS OF THE MARINERS' MUSEUM.

September, but says nothing about what is on hand at the time, so our captain has sent for three 40 Gal. Barrels to have on hand. That is enough to last us one Year. I hope the Government will catch him at it some way, and make him trouble. I hope he will get his deserts yet, before the War is over. . . ."

But Jeffers would not have been the only ship commander to take one last opportunity to stock the spirit lockers, and once the grog law went into effect it became fairly common for captains to ask their surgeons to prescribe a gill or two to each man for medicinal use—usually on a diagnosis of "exhaustion" from impressive effort on deck.

Dear Martha

. . . I do not wounder you are worid at what you read in the Papers . . . about the doings of the Monitor, but they are all bosh. We have not had our Anchor up, Fired a Gun, or been of the least use or service except to act as a scare crow, for most one month. It is all absurd to talk of the Monitor taking her usual morning excursion. . . .

You see I send you some money, which is more than you have paid out for me, and I will send you more the next time I write. I hope you will send me those things as soon as you get the Lettor, and wate for the Sunday Paper, as I have two of the Locks spoke for already and should not wonder if I had to send for more. I shall have to have some more silk, as what you have sent I have sold, and have more saved for my self . . . I want 5 Skeins of each, Red, White, & Blue, and the ballance Black.

I suppose you think I am a good deal of trouble, but you must recollect you are one of the firm Geo. S. Geer & Wife, and I give you all We make — even the Babys.

— AUGUST 13, 1862

I suppose you think I am a good deal of trouble, but you must recollect you are one of the firm Geo. S. Geer & Wife, and I give you all We make—even the Babys.

. . . We sent a Boat on Shore yesterday and killed a nice young Stear that was the property of a Doctor in the Rebel Army. I had some Beef Stake for breakfast, and will have Rost Beef for Dinner, and we had good Beef Soup for dinner yesterday. So you see I am getting fed pretty well at presant, only I miss Bread & Butter, and Milk for my Coffee. You know they are the things I am most fond of. Green Corn we have in great abundance, and will, I presume, as long as it last, as there is a field here of 50 Achors

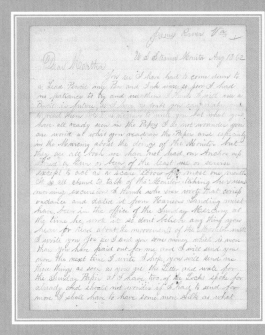

which will go to waste as there is no one to harvest it. Our . . . officers say sence the Government past the law to alow the Army and navy to live off of the Enemy that they are bound to live well as long as they can find any thing on Shore. . . .

Our Captain is going to do something he thinks is smart. The new law about Liquor says no liquor shall be brot on any Government Vessel after the 1st of September, but says nothing about what is on hand at the time, so our captain has sent for three 40 Gal. Barrels to have on hand. That is enough to last us one Year. I hope the Government will catch him at it some way, and make him trouble. I hope he will get his deserts yet, before the War is over. . . .

Your Loving
George

On August 14 McClellan at last issued orders to his commanders and the march back to Fort Monroe began. For the thousands of men who took the roads south that day and the next, and for the miles of wagon trains, the movement attracted more attention among the enemy than aboard the Union ships lying off Harrison's Bar in the James. Confederates did not directly observe the retreating columns, but suspected the withdrawal nonetheless. On the *Monitor*, George Geer learned of the march the first night it was under way, and misinterpreted it entirely. Paymaster Keeler returned from Hampton Roads on August 15, mentioning "Great movements in the army," but even he failed to recognize that they confirmed his speculation of three days before.[13]

Geer suspected another advance on Richmond by land and river. He assumed that the flocks of steamers off the landing were there to supply and support both the army and navy, and that many of the wooden craft might be sacrificed to the underwater mines upriver.

"The Lieutenant has just this moment informed me that after to day there would not be any more males leve her[e] for Fifteen days," he informed his wife on August 15. "I suppose we are to moove on Richmond, as

I learned last evening that the Army were mooving. So things look very much like it. Yesterday all the Gun Boats had large Numbers painted on their Smoke Pipes, which I presume is the manner they will moove up the River. I hear we are not to be in the advance, but will be held as a reserve to come up in case the Richmond should come out. So you may have no worryment about me, as other Vessels will take the lead, and if there is any blowing up it will be some other Vessel than the Monitor."

Recognizing a mortar schooner like those David Dixon Porter had used against the Mississippi forts below New Orleans, Geer also speculated that they would be employed against the batteries at Drewry's Bluff.

Maybe anticipation of a new commander distracted the *Monitor* crew from alternative explanations of the scenes they were witnessing. Commander Thomas H. Stevens had been ordered to relieve Lieutenant Jeffers the week before, but he did not reach his new ship until August 18.

"I have some news to tell you," Geer wrote gleefully. "We are to have a new Captain, and we expect him on board to day. His name is

Stephens, and he has been in Command of the Mohaska. Our Capt. is going on Ordinance duty. I think the Government have found out what I have known some time: that is, that he is half sesesh and is not fit to be in command any way. What our new Captain is, I cannot say, but hear he is a very intemperate man but a good Union man and a good Fighting man. He is a native of Virginia—."

In fact Stevens was a native of Connecticut, but to the *Monitor* sailors it wouldn't have mattered if he had come from Mars. Paymaster Keeler, a temperance supporter, lamented the news that Stevens "has the reputation of taking a glass too much occasionally, the curse of the navy," but even so welcomed the change.

"I can assure you we parted from him without many regrets," wrote Keeler when the gouty Jeffers limped off the deck. "He is a person of a good deal of scientific attainment, but brutal, selfish, & ambitious."[14] Geer concurred completely.

On the following day the last soldier in the Army of the Potomac left the camp at Harrison's Landing. As General McClellan told the story to his wife the following evening, he was that last soldier. Swarms of ships had steamed downriver (a Confederate lieutenant counted 108 of them), and that night the Confederates on the south side of the James reported that the enemy was gone from their front and had built no campfires on the other bank. Only ten ships remained off the bar on August 16: the *Monitor*, five wooden gunboats, and four schooners. The Peninsula Campaign was over.

all enquiring friends This is very hard trying to write setting on the floor with a piece of Board for a Desk Dont fail to write me every Sunday and Wednesday Your Husband George

soday in the ... Friday morning every ... Ship was put in th... and we watched

Seven

NEWPORT NEWS

DESPITE THE ARMY'S DEPARTURE, the gunboats lingered off Harrison's Bar. General Lee began moving the rest of his army north once McClellan's withdrawal was confirmed, carrying the war to the enemy, but for a while longer the Union navy retained control of the lower James River. The Confederate ironclad *Richmond* still posed an exaggerated threat to the Federals, and as the last brigades of the Army of the Potomac marched toward Fort Monroe, the *Monitor* and the rest of the squadron stood guard against any waterborne interdiction. In his first letter after the withdrawal, Geer revealed that the Union sailors were even less well informed of McClellan's movements than were the authorities at Richmond.

Dear Wife

. . . I wrote you in my last that the Armey had mooved on towards Richmond, but I have sence found I was mistaken. They were shiped on Vessels and have gon, I dont know where but suppose to reinforce Pope. So we are left to our selves to finish out the Summer here. I hardly think the Gun Boats will make any advance on Fort Darling now that the Armey are not going to moove up with us. I am completely pussled. I dont know what to make of the moovement, and hope the enemy are the same.

. . . Our new Captain has not arived yet, although our Captain lookes for him every moment and is ancious to have him come so he can get away. And we are all ancious to see him go. So there is no love lost.

All our Gun Boats have come down from above, so the Enemy have all the River above this.

You may send me one Ounce of Black Silk besides what I wrote for before, as there is no Silk in the Ship and none of them got what they sent for by Express.

. . . I came very near freezing where I slept last night. It was a regular NY September night. . . .

Yours,

George

On August 18 Lieutenant Jeffers began his journey back to Washington and ordnance duty. In his place came Commander Thomas H. Stevens, a more experienced and affable officer. First Assistant Engineer Isaac Newton, the acting chief engineer, departed two days later to oversee construction of some of the new ironclads on the ways back in New York. Despite having earned his engineer yeoman's position at Newton's recommendation, George Geer no longer considered the senior engineer a particular friend of his, but he did feel that he held the confidence of the next officer in the engine room, Second Assistant Engineer Albert Campbell, who assumed the role of acting chief.[1]

The squadron lay off a desolate shore now, with only the river between the ships and the enemy inland. Thus isolated from friends and forage the sailors felt vulnerable; when the turret of the *Monitor* jammed, the engineer department worked furiously to free it even when no action loomed.

U.S. Steamer Monitor
James River Aug 20 62

Dear Wife

. . . We have had two changes sence I wrote you on Sunday. On Monday our new Captain came on board and our old one left, and on Tuesday a new Engineer came and brot orders for Newton to go to New York at once and gave the charge of the Engines to Mr. Campbell. We were all very glad of the changes. Our new Captain, I wrote you, was a native of Virginia but I was mistaken. He is a native of South Carolina [sic], and so far appears like a perfect Gentleman and is very kind to us all.

NEWPORT NEWS

Our new Engineer, Mr. Campbell, I have often written you, was my Engineer and the one I liked best of any one in the Ship. So we are all very much pleased with the changes. What the new Engineer is I do not know, or care very much, as he has very little to do with me, and if he did it would make very little diferance as long as Campbell is Chief.

I am very much puzzled to know where the Armey went. They went off so quick and so misteriously we can form no idea of where they went to, but I suppose you know by this time if the Papers dare publish it. But if they have not, you may depend it means something, and I should not be surprised if some of the Rebels got very badly hurt before McClellan gets through with them.

. . . I have had to stop about twenty times sence I commenced this, to run to the store room for something. The reason was that our Tower got Stuck and would not turn, but the reason was that we put som Packing under it while in Hampton Road and it had become Rotten and roled up in a wad as hard as a stone, and in such a place it would not let the Tower turn. But we have it out, and she is working like a Top.

. . . Our Green Corn and Fresh Beef left us when the Armey left, as we dare not send a Boat on Shore sence the Armey left, as the Rebel Pickets are all around us and watch every moove.

I received a Lettor from Gilbert yesterday. It was a coppy of one he sent to Mr. Newton, asking him to recommend me as an Engineer, but Newton did not get it untill this morning, and as he did not get up untill 7 ½ oclock and the Boat came for him at 8 he did not have time to answer it, or say anything to me about it. I suppose he will answer it from NY when he arrives there, but I expect very little favor from him. . . .

Your Husband
George

The arrival of Commander Stevens restored the atmosphere of peace and camaraderie that had prevailed in the early days of the *Monitor*. Stevens did seem to appreciate the effect of liquor, as Geer noted the next time the coal bunkers had to be filled, but he also scorned the haughty airs that had so alienated Lieutenant Jeffers from officers and crewmen alike. Where Jeffers had clung to his cabin as to a castle, Stevens was not averse to calling his paymaster and surgeon into a boat for a fishing expedition.[2]

Geer's next letter, dated August 24, reveals a curious new fact—that the *Monitor* did not end its days wearing the black paint apparent in its only series of photographs. He and another sailor painted the entire vessel a "light lead" color that sounds similar to the battleship gray of steel ships in the next century.

In his free time Geer was managing his mercantile sideline and corresponding with his wife about ordinary news from home and life aboard ship—sharing the tidbits of daily existence that helped bind them during his absence. Reading Geer's letter of August 24, it is clear that Martha had told him of a woman named Kate (presumably her brother William's wife) who had become pregnant. Geer's teasing response, perhaps cryptic to modern readers, was earthy and intimate:

"I am sorry about Kate," he wrote, adding, "You may have no fear for your self, as I will stop in Philadelphia on my way home and get over the worst of it. I suppose you are willing, aint you?"

This gentle bit of humor—that, with Martha's permission, he might spare her the possibility of another pregnancy by stopping over in Philadelphia to alleviate his accumulated desires—seems to underscore their mutual trust in a setting in which many codes of Victorian society were doubtless regularly broken.

We like our Captain very much. He is not such an old Wind Bag as Jeffers was, and I think when the time comes for more Fighting he will do all than [sic] can be done to Give the Monitor a good name and Punish the Rebels.

— AUGUST 24, 1862

Dear Wife

I have received from you sence I wrote you last two Papers on Friday, the Mercury and the Times, and to day the Times and Sun and your ever welcom Lettor. . . .

I am sorry you could not send me the Silk before you went *[to Troy]*. I want it very much. You do not say you received the money ($6.00), but I suppose you have as it was in that Lettor. I stated the males would be stoped, but for some reason they were not and I get your Lettors regular. The money must have come to you in a very good time. I suppose you will not be in NY to draw your money the first of Sept., but it will make no diferance as you can draw the two months, or $30, on the first of October, if you can get along. I have $3 I will send you if you want any time, as I have no use for it here.

. . . We like our Captain very much. He is not such an old Wind Bag as Jeffers was, and I think when the time comes for more Fighting he will do all than *[sic]* can be done to Give the Monitor a good name and Punish the Rebels. I think from what I have seen of him that he will pleas us as well as Worden did. In fact, sence we have got clear of Jeffers and Newton it seams like another Ship, and the men are bettor natured.

Yesterday we Coaled Ship. We took in 30 Ton and commenced at 7 oclock and were through by 11 oclock. It used to take all day when Jeffers was here, but this

Captain had Grog served to the men and they were so pleased they worked like

Beavers. Anything of that sort goes fa[r]ther with a Saylor than a presant of $5 would.

We had up Steam on Friday and took a Cruse down the River some 8 or 10 miles

to let the Capt. see how the Ship would work, and I must say I never saw her work so

well before. The Capt. would go up and attack Fort Darling alone if the Comodore

would let him.

We have made some alteration in the Color of this Vessel. We have painted her a

very light Lead Color. I had a good pull at Painting her. Two of us done the whole of it.

I am sorry about Kate. You may have no fear for your self, as I will <u>stop</u> in <u>Philadelphia</u> on my way home and <u>get over the worst of it.</u> I suppose you are willing, aint you?

. . . I want you to send me any Paper that has an account of the Launch of the new Monitor, which you wrote me would take place on the 25, Tomorrow. We are watching her very clost, and any thing that looks like her completion is haled with Joy, as we know we will not be relieved untill one of them take our place.

We are in Commission Six Month[s] to day. I dont think there ever lived a man could say he had been on Iron Six Months and never steped on the Ground in that time.

. . . Write me what Gilbert says about my getting an appointment, if any thing new has turned up sence he wrote me last.

. . . I am going to visit the Galena and will have to Close. . . .

Your
George

Impatient with inactivity, Commodore Wilkes pondered another expedition up the Appomattox River—to the horror of those who had made the earlier pilgrimage there. On the evening of August 27 the entire squadron chugged up the James to City Point and dropped anchor.[3]

Perhaps hearing belatedly of the battle of Cedar Mountain, that evening George Geer wrote to his wife that he had heard that Pope's new Army of Virginia had been repulsed. "I hear it rumered that Pope has been driven back," he informed her, "but I have seen no later Paper than the one you sent me. I do not know if it is true, but hope it is."

As it happened, Pope stood then on the verge of yet another defeat at Second Manassas, and Geer's hopeful comment illustrates the complicated politics of the late summer of 1862. General Pope represented the radical Republicans and the abolition faction against George McClellan's more conservative aim of restoring the Union as it was, with slavery intact. Pope rode under the standard of total war, promising to wage his campaign against all Confederates, in uniform and out; McClellan fought Lee's army alone, while respecting the property of the civilian population. Geer's admission suggests that he, like many other War Democrats, would have preferred to see Pope's army sacrificed to satisfy a political preference. Pope himself suspected as much, and mutual mistrust played a significant role in his undoing.

U.S. Steamer Monitor Jas. River
City Point Aug 27 1862

Dear Wife

Here we are again at our old place, City Point. We lay about one mile above the point. We have only been here about one hour, and none of us know if we are going to stay here or are going up to give Fort Darling another bombarding. All we know is that the Comodore made signals for the Fleet to get under way and we did so, and followed the Flag Ship up to this point. He is something like McClellan—keeps every thing to him self, although I do not see the use of it as there is very little chance of the Enemy having any communication with us to find out our moovements.

Sence I wrote you last I received two Ledgers and one Sun from you, but nothing in them. So I wrote yesterday to Jonny and sent him $200 to get me 2 oz. of Silk. There is none in the Ship, and I can sell every Skein for 4&5¢ pr. Skein. I sold the Locks, one for 4/- [4 bits, or 50 cents] and one with the Hinges and screws for 100, and the other is sold for 4/- as soon as I can get the Screws. I wrote to Jonny for them. I have a custimer for another set [of] Lock and Hinges at $100 as soon as I can get them for him. . . .

I shall not get a head much with my account this month, as I have drawn $10 Cash and shall have to draw about $8 in Cloathing as it is so Cold I have had to put on Under Cloathing, and I found my Drawers were worn out so I drew two pair. They are Blue Flannel, and quite warm. I think I have been very saving on Cloathing. I dont think I have drawn $25 in the time I have been Shiped, and I can get along for the next three months without drawing any thing. I am very sorry I took off my Under Cloathing. I wish I had worn them all Summer, and I think if I had I would not have had a tuch of the Rumatism. I will be very careful not to try the experiment of taking them off again.

The Gambling still keeps going, though some of the worst ones have lost all the[y] had, and every body is glad. One boy who only had 50¢ when he commenced has won $40. He is the Youngest boy in the Ship, and it is fun to see him take the money from some of the old gamblers. . . .

Your Husband
George

> I am very sorry I took off my Under Cloathing. I wish I had worn them all Summer, and I think if I had I would not have had a tuch of the Rumatism. I will be very careful not to try the experiment of taking them off again.
>
> — AUGUST 27, 1862

The Appomattox expedition came to nothing. The Navy Department ordered Wilkes to transfer his little squadron to Aquia Creek, a tributary of the Potomac, in order to cooperate with the army that was gathering near Fredericksburg. The ships lay overnight off City Point, but on the morning of August 28 their anchors came up for the return trip. As they started downstream, the last one in line drew fire from pickets on shore and opened up with its little deck guns in return. The *Monitor* lumbered back around to help, and in the final volleys of the navy's Peninsula Campaign a plantation at the tip of City Point felt the effects of the ironclad's eleven-inch guns. The home of Dr. Eppes, who would serve as an involuntary host of Ulysses Grant three winters hence, sat on the bluff at the junction of the two rivers; the *Monitor*'s Dahlgrens lobbed a few shells into the gleaming white structure, then the portals fell closed and the prow turned back toward Harrison's Landing.

The next day the squadron weighed anchor to abandon the James River, with the *Monitor* trailing her sisters in case the *Richmond* should come up from behind. Commodore Wilkes took most of the ships with him up the Potomac, leaving the *Monitor* at Newport News to guard the mouth of the James. Almost immediately the engineer department started overhauling the machinery, and George Geer took his first jaunt ashore in more than six months. It was the beginning of September, the time when Virginia peaches are ripening. In customary fashion Geer not only enjoyed himself but tried to turn a little profit in fruit.[4]

Newport News Va Sept 1 1862

Dear Wife

. . . You see by the date that we are at last out of the infernal James River and once more on Salt Water. I wrote you last on Wednesday, and on Thursday we were ordered to get up Steam and follow the Flag Ship. I thought shure when I saw her steam past us that we were all going to make an attack on Fort Darling, but we proceeded as far as City Point and anchored. The next morning we got up Anchor and Steamed down as far as Harrisons Landing, and had hardly got our Anchor down when Fireing was herd in the direction of City Pint. We hastened back and found it was our Amanition Schooner in Tow of a small Tug they were Fireing at, so we gave them about ½ Doz Shell, which soon sent them flying. We next turned our attention to a very fine house that was the property of a Colonel in the Rebel Army and has been the resort of Sharp Shooters and Pickets for some time. So all the Boats that had come up took a hand at nocking it to pieces. I stood on our Deck, and I could hear the Bricks of the Chimney tumble down, so you may know we were pretty clost, and I could see the Shell go through the houses, and when one Exploded the pieces would fly in every direction. After we had used the House as a Target long enough we through one of our Fire Shell in to it and set it on fire. We then went down to Harrisons Landing again, and staid untill the next morning, when we were ordered to Steam side of the Flag Ship for Orders. Our orders were that the whole fleet was going down the river and we were to bring up the Rear and see nothing was left behind. We came down, but the others were so much faster we were soon left behind. We stoped and took the men and their things out of the Light Houses, and got down here on Saturday morning.

Our Engineer got permission from the Comodore to have our fires out for 24 hours, so we pulled them about 10 oclock, and from that time untill Sunday noon every body had all they could do repairing the Boilers and diferant parts that could not be when Steam was on. At 12 oclock Steam was started again, and [all] of us but the regular watch was relieved.

After dinner the Lieutenant called us and read off a list of half the Crew who were to be allowed to go on Shore, and I was one of the luckey ones allthough the rest will have their liberty next Sunday. So you may know I had no time to write, and hardly time to dress before the boat was ready and [a]Shore we went. There is some 2500 Sick and Wounded Solgers and about as many Well ones. As soon as we got on Shore all hands went looking for Liquor but two of us, so we started for a Strole in the

Country. We went untill we ment the Pickets, and after talking to them some time we finally got past them and went some two miles down the Road to the Fortress. We came to a house and tride to buy some Peaches, so we bought about three Pecks from them for one Dollar. We have not sold any yet, as they are not ripe enough to be good and we are going to keep them untill they are. We shall sell them for 2/- [25 cents] pr. Doz., and have $2.00 spoken for, but I do not think we will sell more than that and [will] keep the ballance for our selves. We will have a good feast of the ballance. . . .

We had a hard time car[ry]ing our Peaches down to the Boat, and our Feet were Blistered. We were arrested by the Pickets when we came in, and taken to head Quarters, but the officer told us to go on; it was all right.

. . . I was very glad to hear you had bought Coal with the money I sent you. It will save you running to the Grocery, and save money. How is your stove? Did you think to get any thing for it while you was up?

Give Willey a kiss for Papa. Give my Love to Every body.

Your
George

While the *Monitor* had been tossing shells at the Eppes plantation, Stonewall Jackson stood near the old Bull Run battlefield where he had earned his nickname, preparing a bloody greeting for John Pope and the Army of Virginia. Fighting erupted that evening and continued for three days, ending when Pope's army fled back to the outskirts of Washington. His retreat forced the evacuation of the new base at Aquia Creek, and the refugees gathered near the capital. Next, Lee's army marched north into Maryland, throwing Washington, Baltimore, and Harrisburg into a panic, but George McClellan started after him with his old Army of the Potomac augmented by the battered divisions that had followed Pope. Suddenly, the James River seemed relatively unimportant and forces on both sides enjoyed the lull.

Newport News provided the *Monitor*'s crew with the most pleasant interlude of their sojourn aboard the ironclad. From there the war lay far away, and their anchorage came to resemble a shoreside resort. Some men took advantage of the relaxed discipline, and for one enlisted man the exuberance proved fatal: in a drunken rage, the wardroom steward (not Geer's friend Daniel Moore) attempted to murder the paymaster's steward, and lost his life in the process.[5] Officers tested their new commander's benevolence as well, and Geer learned that Engineer Newton had made good on his promise to put in a good word in support of Geer's quest for a promotion. These and other events he chronicled in a long letter home.

U.S. Steamer Monitor
Newport News Sept 3 1862

Dear Wife

Wednesday again, and as usual I am trying to make up a Lettor that will be welcom to you. I have not received anything from Johny yet, but shall look for the Silk in the male to day, which for some reason we do not get untill 7 oclock in the Evening, although the male arives at Fortress Monroe early in the morning and the Boat makes three trips each day from the Fortress up here. It is only nine miles.

We are having very fine times here, and you know we should have after our Six Months of misery. This Captain is as good a man as Worden was, and he gives the men every thing he can, reasonably. He says we can have money any time we have any coming to us, and the Paymaster told me he should serve out money to all hand that wanted any in a day or two, so I may be able to send you some in my next Lettor, or soon at any rate. I am now spending some money here for Bread & Butter on shore, although I have not spent yet any more than I have made. My share of profit on the Peaches was 6/- *[75 cents]* besides as many as we could eat, so we done very well. . . .

I receved a Lettor from Mr. Newton. He says he saw Mr. Fox, the Assistant Secretary of the Navy, in New York, and he told him he was going to order the Monitor to ~~NY~~ Washington in a fiew days. We hear that Capt. Worden is to have command of one of the new Iron Clads, and has asked permission to have his old Crew with him. I hope it is true, as that would take us to NY, and his Vessel will not be ready untill the middle of November, so we would be some time in N York.

The Officers have riged up one of our Cutter Boats with a Sail, and last evening a party of us took a sail around the reck of the Cumberland. She lays in the same place she Sank; only her Mast are out of water. It is hard to believe there are the bodys of so many poor Saylors laying in their Watery Grave in that Ship, and what a sight it will be when they rase here [sic], which the Government will do as soon as the War is over. Her Sails are still on the Yards—every thing as she was when she Sank. We were gon from the Ship about two hours, and the wind died away so we had to row back.

It was just dusk when we got back, and we had been on board hardly five moments when one of the men Jumped or Roled over board and was drownded. He was the Wardroom Stewart, and was very fond of liquor, it seams. He had been on shore to buy things for the Wardroom when he got hold of a bottle of Whisky and drank the whole of it. He was so crazy he took up an Ax and threw [it] at a Colord Boy, which if it had have hit him would have killed him. The Captain had him put out forward of the Pilot house, away from any body, but did not have any Irons put on him. The Lieutenant was away at the time, but when he came on board he told the Captain he was a bad man when in Liquor, and he had bettor put the Irons on him. As soon as he saw the Irons he became as Crazy as poseable, and it took 4 men to hold him while the Irons were put on him. They had hardly left him when he made a spring and eather fell or roled off the side. As both his hands and feet were Ironed of corse he could make no exertion to save him self if he wanted to, and he must have went under the Vessel, as the tide was running very strong. We had boats grapling for him most of the night, but could not find him. He always said he had a Wife and daughter in Calaforna, but he could not have been much help or comfort to them, and he will not be much looss to them, as he never sent any money to them, but Gambled it away.

We are in a bad way here about sleeping. It is to Cold to sleep on deck, and the Mosquetoes will eat us up if we Sleep down below. But a fiew such Cold nights as last night will clear them out.

. . . Our Officers are having very fine times. Some of them are away every day. Two of them went to Norfolk yesterday, and did not get back last night. The Captain does not like it much, and he will not let them go again, unless they can give a good Excuse.

. . . I think if I stay in the Navy this Winter I can send you money enough so you can live very comfortable. I hope I will get liberty long enough to have my Teath repaired, as they are so bad I cannot eat any thing hard. Was the tooth you had pulled a front Tooth, and does it show bad?

. . . Tell Willey Papa wants to see his little boy very bad, and wants Willey to sleep with to keep him warm this Winter. I dont suppose Gilley will know me. How I would like to see if the little fellow would Cry if I took him. . . .

I hardly think there will be any draft in N York; I hope not. Send some Paper Sunday, I dont care which. I want you to send me a Harpers Magasine: it has some pictures of the building of the Monitor— I mean the September number.

With all Love I remain

Your George

When Commander Stevens authorized the paymaster to dole out funds to the crew at Newport News, Geer's business enterprises boomed. With money in their pockets, his shipmates began to feed their main leisure diversion through him, buying up brilliant thread for the intricate embroidery with which they decorated their clothing. The *Monitor*'s berth deck also harbored thieves— Geer's own government issue handkerchiefs had been pilfered—fueling the demand for hinges and locks.

The success of his commercial ventures and the release of some of his pay alleviated much of Geer's concerns for his family's financial situation. It did not relieve his homesickness, though, and he remained preoccupied with any topic—the chances of a trip to the Washington Navy Yard, for instance, or the launching of one of the navy's new monitor-class vessels from New York— that held the promise of a chance for him to come home.

Dear Wife

Your Lettor and the Silk came to hand all right, and I sold all the Silk but Six skeins I kept for my self, and the colored Silk. . . . I got for what Silk I sold $3oo, so you see I make very well off of it, besides having what I want to use my self. . . .

The Lock, Hinges, and Screws came all right. I sold the Lock as soon as I took it out of the paper for 6/-, [75 cents] and sold the one I had on my own Box with the hinges for $1.00, and have another set promised at $1.00, so I shall want you to send me three Locks and two set Hinges with the Screws, complete. . . .

I want you to buy me a good, large, heavy Black Silk . . . Handkerchief. These we get here cost $1.oo each and are very poor, and are all precisely alike, so someone— I cannot say who—thinks it cheeper to steel than buy, and I have had two stolen from me. As they are all alike, there is no swaring to one, or is it safe to accuse one of Stealing. . . .

I suppose you see the inclosed $10. I drew from the Paymaster $25oo this morning, and have some 4 or 5 Dollars besides, so I shall send you $25oo by sending part in each Lettor. I hope none of it will get lost or stolen in the P.O. I do not think I will send any more untill I hear you have received this, as this will provide for all your pressing wants. You must use your own judgment about the money. When you get it all if you can spare some of it pay Rachel some on what I am in her debt. I think you had bettor keep it to your self that you have got any money from me, at least untill you have your own wants supplide. You must use your own judgement is the best advise I can give you. Sence I have got the money I am not in so much of a hurry for us to go to Washington, and I have not felt so contented sence I have been in the Ship. It seams to be a great relief to me to know I can send you some money.

You dont know how glad I was to get a lock of Hare from the Heads of those two little tow heads. How I do want to see them, or even a picture of them. . . .

Give my Love to Rach and all hand[s]. I must stop or loose to days male, so with much love I remain

Your Husband
George

Early in September two pieces of bad news arrived at the *Monitor*. In the first instance, week-old newspapers and journals read by the ship's officers evidently brought details of Pope's defeat at Second Bull Run and the Confederate invasion of Maryland.[6] "... I see very bad news in the paper, but I hope it will be only temporary," Geer observed in his letter of September 10—although just a few weeks earlier Geer had wished that Pope might meet with disaster. But with McClellan once more in command, Geer perhaps thought the Union armies would soon rebound to victory.

Even more important to Geer and other men of the *Monitor* was the discovery that Commander Stevens had been relieved of his duties.

"I have learned some very bad news sence I commenced this Lettor," Geer told Martha. "... [O]ur Captain is to leve us tomorrow and take command of a new Ship, and a Captain by the name of Bankhead is to take command of us. We are all very sorry, both Officers and men, but we can only hope for the best. It seams as though it was imposeable for the Monitor to keep a good Captain, but I will hope for the best. This man coming may be a good one, and I will not condem him untill we have given him a trial."

Commander John P. Bankhead.
From the Collections of The Mariners' Museum.

In Stevens's place came Commander John P. Bankhead, a native of South Carolina and a cousin of at least one Confederate major general. More Southern-born naval officers displayed national loyalty than did their army counterparts; Bankhead was one who had remained with the Union despite family ties. In due course he would be evaluated by the ironclad's crew, but three days after his arrival George Geer related to

Martha the story of Stevens's emotional leavetaking. Uncorroborated by other sources, it remains as one man's recounting of events that clearly shook the tranquillity aboard the *Monitor* in the dog days of summer 1862.

". . . Our new Captain has been with us only three days, and I cannot tell much about him. He says he was only ordered here for a short time. I hope the Government will get some body here bom [by and] by that will suit. We had a very affecting time before Stevens left us. The reason was this. When this Captain came here he told Stephens the reason the Government took this Vessel from him was for Drunkenness—that the day the Iron Sides was here her Captain came on board the Monitor with the Captain of an English Man of War and some half Dozen other Officers and som three or four Ladies, and he was so Drunk he was not able to entertain them. It is a damd Lie. I noticed him particular that day, and saw he was slightly under the infulance of Liquor, but by no means Drunk. In fact, two of [us] ware talking about it at the time and wondering which had the most—our Captain or the Captain of the Iron Sides. As soon as we learned the caus of his removal the Crew was mad enough, and so were the other Officers. The Officers at once drew up a Lettor of respect and presented it to him, and sent a Lettor to Washington deniing the charge and asking to have him restored to the Monitor again. The Crew then drew up a Lettor and every man signed it, and I was one of the Committy to present it to him. When we presented it to him he could not help Crying. He called us all togather and thanked the Crew and made a very kind and affecting Speach. There was more eyes than his own that were moist, and when he got on the Tug he got 9 as hearty chears as ever a man had."

While enlisted men were customarily prohibited from drinking intoxicating liquor on duty except under supervision, such as when grog was issued, officers of the navy and the army drank with impunity on duty or even in the midst of battle, and they frequently ran afoul of courts-martial as a result. The question usually considered by a court-martial or a court of inquiry was not whether the defendant was under the influence of spirits, but the precise extent of his intoxication. Colonel Dixon S. Miles, for instance, was found to have been drunk while commanding a division at the first battle of Bull Run in 1861, but was allowed to retain his rank and was eventually placed in command of the garrison at Harpers Ferry; even as Fireman Geer wrote the foregoing words, the alcoholic Miles was being surrounded by Stonewall Jackson's troops, who would kill him and capture his entire command.[7]

In other respects, life on the ironclad simply went along—Geer the merchant diligently orchestrating his hardware and notions business, Geer the husband and father longing for the company of his family, and Geer the underemployed sailor enjoying meager comforts while the *Monitor* continued to wait at Newport News. Excerpts from his September 10 letter to his "Dear Wife" tidily summarize Geer's days:

"Your kind and welcom Lettor came to hand this morning, togather with the Papers and Soap. . . . I have plenty of soap at presant. . . . When we came down the River we brot the Light House keepers and all their things. One of them had 8 bars of brown soap. It was furnished to him by the Government, and as long as it was bublick property I thought I would fall in love with two bars. So you see they will last me some time. . . ."

"In your Lettor you say that you are loansum and wish bad to see me [but] I think not more than I want to see you. It seems as though I think of you more and more every day. In fact, my thoughts are on you continuly, and if we go to Washington I dont know what will keep me from coming to NY. It will be only becaus it is uterly imposeable. How I long to see those two little Chubs. I think of them and their Mother day and night.

". . . I have chum[m]ed in with two other men and we buy things to eat, or rather I do; they each pay their share, and I do the buying and Cooking. We have on hand at presant one Ham, 16 lbs., 2 Loavs Bread, and 1 lb. Cheese, so you see we are not going to starve. I had 3 good Carlina Potatoes for my Breakfast. I had them given to me by the Wardroom Cook, and I can tell you they tasted bully as I had some Butter to put in them. . . ."

Geer took full advantage of his free time at this peaceful anchorage to engage in more speculation. He tried to profit a few cents on everything his wife sent him, usually with success.

"Some of these fools would buy any thing if they only had the money," he said in his September 13 letter. "As a specamin of what a fool Jack [Tar] is, when they was on shore they gave the sutlers $3<u>00</u> for Quart Bottles of Whiskey that any one can buy in NY for 40¢ pr. Gal. $3<u>00</u> pr. bottle is about $15<u>00</u> [sic] pr. Gallon, so you may have some idea of how Jack spends his money, and it was not buying one bottle, but by the Dozen."

Geer even began to dream about putting together enough cash to move his family from their New York apartment to a farm—a possibility that would lie far beyond his resources for years to come.

—⋅—

On Sunday, September 14, Geer joined another sailor and several officers in a foraging expedition several miles up the James River. Searching for peaches or other provisions, they found trees stripped bare by (Geer supposed) "damd nigers," who had their own enterprises selling fruit to the army. The party also found once gracious plantation houses burned to the ground.

"We went up and down the River some two or three miles and could not see one house standing," Geer later wrote with dismay. "The 7th NYV, Blenkers Regiment, burned every house that was empty, and I got more ide[a] of the terrors of War last Sunday than I ever had before, to see the Ruins of what ware apparently fine Brick Cuntry Residences, and to think that they were burned as so much rubish simply becaus they were empty looked awfull, and I could not help looking and wondering what had become of the people who once inhabited them, and wonder if they ever dremped [dreamt] that their happy homes would come to Ashes."

Geer was probably mistaken in blaming Colonel Louis Blenker for the arson. Blenker actually had commanded the 8th New York Infantry, informally known as the 1st German Rifles because the regiment contained so many German-born men. The 7th New York, which Geer blamed for the home burnings, also carried a large number of German names on its roster and had served in the same region for the better part of a year. Blenker's regiment, along with the 7th New York and others, had occupied Newport News just six weeks into the war, ranging eight miles inland from their base at Fort Monroe. The gutted houses that so shocked Geer probably lay around the mouth of Watts Creek, which a raiding party of the 7th New York visited a second time on July 12, 1861.[8]

Geer's irritation at the needless destruction reflected the attitude of a conservative War Democrat—which he indeed seemed to be. Like his new commanding officer Bankhead, Geer favored George McClellan as a military leader and cringed at such disrespect for private property even in a disloyal state.[9]

As Geer was writing to Martha about "happy homes . . . come to Ashes," George McClellan launched his first and only attack against the Army of Northern Virginia, striking Lee in three separate assaults along Antietam Creek in western Maryland. In the bloodiest single day of the war he failed to crush the Confederate army, which numbered barely half as many as his own forces, but he stunned the enemy and Lee withdrew across the Potomac the next night. That ended the immediate threat to the capital, and apparently quelled Geer's concerns about the fate of his country's cause.

The battle of Antietam, for all of its lost opportunities, gave President Lincoln enough of a battlefield victory that he dared announce

Seven Months to day I have been in the Navy, and it may be some time yet before I see you again. I had very little idea that I should be away from you over Six Months when I parted with you. I thought the War would be over in that time, but it is no nearer over than it was when I shiped. . . . We finaly gave up looking for Peaches and went to Fishing for Crabs. They are very plenty here, and we soon had as many as we wanted, but they are no rarety as we can catch them from the Vessel any time, and I often when I am hungry take the net and in two moments catch two or three fine Crabs and clap them in the Oven as soon as they are out of the Water, and it is Cruel Funn to see them crall around in the hot oven, but they are soon Cooked and Devoured.

—SEPTEMBER 14, 1862

his Emancipation Proclamation, linking the political aim of reunion with the moral effect of a crusade for freedom. While the proclamation elevated the international perception of Northern goals and secured the support of abolitionists at home, it alienated conservative constitutionalists like Geer. Lincoln did not formally issue the proclamation until September 22, but Geer's letters from that period remained curiously silent on the subject.

U.S. Steamer Monitor
Newport News Sept 21 62

Dear Wife

. . . I have been living high lately, as I have written you before, and every one says how fat you are getting, and I can tell you I feel as strong as an Ox and can <u>eat</u> about as much as one. I must stop for a moment, as my Friend Moore the Cook has just handed me a slice of Bread with a piec of Roast Beef on it the size of the Slice—Bully. That hurt my <u>fealings</u>. He often gives me such tit bits. He is a regular damd fool, but I make him think he is a great Cook and make him think I am going to bring him home with me. I may do so, if we both go to NY, as he has been very kind to me, I will say that, and he is a very good Cook.

I went out Sayling on Friday with one of the Officers, and we went to the Cumberland, and I got two Blocks, or Pulleys, and am going to try and make a Ring out of one of the Wheels. The Soldiers have taken most every Block off of her to make Rings of. The Divers were here this week and went down in her, but I could not find out if they saw any bodys in her, but I have no doubt they did. They are going to commence Rasing all the Ships sunk here soon. . . .

Yours in Haste
George

As the Southern summer waned, Geer's letters turned long again, with commentary on the contented mood aboard the *Monitor*, his ever-present business dealings, and occasional intimate exchanges with Martha—whom he was missing more than ever. Evidently she was considering weaning both three-year-old Willey and her younger son, Gilley. That could be a serious decision for a Victorian woman, for nursing a child was the only (however haphazard) means of avoiding ovulation in the nineteenth century; for couples not wishing to practice abstinence, it was the most popular form of birth control. As Geer made clear, he did not intend to abstain if he could make his way home.

> U.S. Steamer Monitor
> *Newport News Sept 24 62*

Dear Wife

. . . It is know *[now]* 8 oclock, and . . . I must say I am as contented as it is poseable for me to be away from my Family. Ever sence Newton and Jeffers left us it seams like another Ship. Every thing goes on so pleasantly: no fault finding, no cross looks from the Officers, and in fact nothing that is anyways unreasonable expected or required of the men. The Saylors growl—some of the old ones that always have— but that is part of them. . . . You would have thought when the Grog was stoped in the Navy that the Cuntry would go to the Dogs to hear them talk. . . . And now you hardly hear Grog mentioned from one week end to another.

The bundle of Papers with the Knife came to hand. . . . The Knife was a very nice one, and I sold it before I had had it five moments for 10/- *[$1.25]* and promised two more. So you may send me two as soon as you pleas. Get the same kind, if you can. . . .

You may wonder why my money is all gon, but I will tell you I have been living pretty well lately, and I have paid $5<u>00</u> you recollect I borrowed and sent you some time ago. So you see I have spent very little foolishly. . . . I find I cannot get along this Winter without a Pair of Boots here, as I will get my feet wet every time I go on Deck when it comes rough weather. The Government only serve out Shoes, so I shall have to buy a pair here or send to NY for them. I was on Shore yesterday, and asked the price, and they Chg $7.00 for a pair of very common Pegg Boots. I want you to ask Jonny or make the enquiry what the price of a Good pair of Sea Boots is. What I mean by sea Boots is these heavy Grained Leather Boots with pretty high Leggs. Any boot maker knows what sea Boots are. If the Price is so I can make any thing I will send you the money and let you send me two or three pair by Express. I am bound to make [money] when ever I have a chance. The boys call me the Specilator, and as long as I have the name I am bound to have the game. . . .

I am glad you are going to put Willey in Pants, and I think it is most time you thought of Weaning that Boy you tell about being such a fine one. . . . It is time he dispenced with Titty Milk and you need have no fear of any <u>consequences</u> after you Wean him, at least untill I come home. . . .

Your Loving
George

By now Geer also began to suspect that the *Monitor* would soon be sent to the Washington Navy Yard. Rather than jinx their luck he nominally discounted the idea, but further remarks about going home for a visit and his allusions to making a personal visit to the assistant secretary of the navy strongly hint that circumstances in the engine room and shipboard scuttlebutt portended the ironclad's departure.

Dear Wife

Your kind and ever welcom Lettor came to hand to day. You say you do not know as the Picture will suit me. I can tell you it does suit me, to a dot. There is only one thing that would please me bettor, and that would be to see the Original. The Picture is all I could ask. It is you as perfect as can be, and I do not think you have altered much. You say I wish I could return the compliment. I wish I could. We had an Artist on board when we were at City Point, but he only took the Crew in a groop and I was sick at the time. He said he would come and take each mans Picture separate, but the Army went away and so did the Artist, and we lost the Opertunity.

You say you are going to wean Gilley. I am glad of it. You will then have a chance to get some flesh on you, and I can give you my word you will not Wean another Baby that I am Father of in one long while. I shall take good care in future not to meet with any <u>axidents,</u> so it is not worth while to save Baby Cloaths as I dont think they will be very handy to have in the house.

. . . The long expected New Iron Sides came in this morning, and is now anchored some half mile from us. She looks very form[id]able, but I believe we could pitch in her and sink her before she could us. At any rate, I am satisfide to be on the Monitor and know what she can stand. But the Iron Sides has yet to be tested and may proove an other Galena. She has come here to relieve us or the Galena—which, we do not know. There was an inspection held by the Chief Engineer of the Minisota of our Engines, but he did not say what he thought of them as he was to hold one on the Galena, and the one that was in the worst condition would be sent home. I hope it will be us, and I will probaly know before I write you again, and perhaps before I mail this Lettor. It would pleas me very much to hear that we are ordered to Washington, but I dare not hope for such good luck.

. . . After you send me the two knives I wish you would send me a set of Lock, Hinges, & Screws, as I have them sold for one Dollar. I see by the Papers that Coal is $7<u>50</u>, and that it will be $12<u>00</u> this Winter: not very encouraging for the Poor. I am very glad you have yours, and that you were able to get it before Coal went up. . . .

I have your Photograph side of me, and have to stop every moment to take a look at you. It makes me home sick to look at it.

. . . I got a Lettor from Gilbert. He is doing nothing for me at presant, but is wating for me to go to Washington when I go there. I will try very hard to get appointed my self. I shall go and see Mr. Fox him self, and urge him very hard to give me an appointment. . . .

Your

Loving Husband

<u>George S. Geer</u>

Geer's instincts proved reliable. The *New Ironsides* had come to take the place of the *Monitor,* and on the last day of September the first of the turreted ironclads started up Chesapeake Bay for Washington, under the tow of a tugboat.[10]

Dear Wife

... this evening to while away
... thought I would write you a few
lines and ... that manner ...
... of the evening but what will
... write about I do not ...
am out of new... all I think
... before ... that I have no might
... I can go to Bed when I like
... and can lay until six if I ... please
... not ... after four and am to ...
... Breakfast and clean ...

Eight

WASHINGTON

THE *MONITOR* TIED UP at the navy yard dock at 9:00 A.M. on George Geer's fourth wedding anniversary, October 3, with the white marble of the unfinished congressional building staring down from Capitol Hill, over the tops of tenements. Fresh earthen forts scarred the landscape. The summer's crop of new three-year regiments, as well as the nine-month troops encouraged by the militia draft, were still bringing floods of new soldiers into the city, and their tents turned the slopes white.

Washington lay more at ease for these forts and tents, but also from the knowledge that the Confederate army had retreated back across the Potomac. McClellan's legions camped quietly between Lee and the capital, and the soldiers enjoyed a long autumn respite from their bloody work of summer.

This dime-sized, souvenir copper token is inscribed "Our Little Monitor" on the front and "1863" on the reverse.
FROM THE COLLECTIONS OF
THE MARINERS' MUSEUM.

Souvenir spoon commemorating the battle between the Monitor *and the "Merrimac." In the bowl, a scene in enamel portays the battle with the inscription "Merrimac and Monitor, March 8, 1862." The front side of the handle bears the inscription "Virginia," the Virginia state seal, and an oyster, a crab, a peanut, and a tobacco plant. A coat of arms with an American eagle appears on the reverse side of the handle. The spoon is five and one half inches long.*
From the Collections of The Mariners' Museum.

The *Monitor* drew massive crowds to the navy yard, and the day after its arrival marine guards opened the gates to the curious hordes. Soldiers by the hundreds, businessmen in broadcloth, women, and children all swarmed aboard the little ship. Troops of women headed down the ladder and entertained themselves in the officers' staterooms; Paymaster Keeler said he found several using his room as a vanity, plying their hair with his comb and brush. Billowing petticoats filled the little passageways, likely delighting the deck hands and engineers who had seen no women at all for many months, let alone glimpse their legs as they climbed the ladders. That afternoon a guard detail had to drive the visitors away from the ship so the officers could eat.

The ironclad was placed in the hands of the yard superintendent on October 5, and went immediately under repair. The unarmed side-wheel steamer *King Philip* lay nearby, unoccupied, so officers and men trundled aboard the relatively spacious decks of that vessel for a few days. Captain Bankhead started away on leave immediately, leaving authorization for the rest of the men to go home for anywhere from two weeks to thirty days. The paymaster stayed behind to settle accounts, but by the beginning of the second week in October the last of the crew had left Washington with several months' worth of pay in their pockets.[1]

An ecstatic George Geer started for New York on the first available train. He came home to a flat he had never seen, on the Canal Street end of narrow, dingy Allen Street. Here rickety tenements leaned precariously against each other. In front of them, many of the occupants took their water from hand pumps on the street. Within another decade, the neighborhood's abundant cheap housing would draw a tidal wave of mostly Jewish immigrants, who would make it their own. A block to the northeast stood Hester Street, with its open-air street markets, and Delancey Street lay three blocks beyond. Wearing the blue flannel uniform that was his only clothing, Geer made his way to 9 Allen Street from the New York train station.

Martha Geer was twenty-four years old when her husband came home on his first furlough. Their son Willey, who was three, may have had difficulty remembering his father. At two, Gilley probably did not remember him at all. Martha's sister, Rachel Hamilton, seems to have

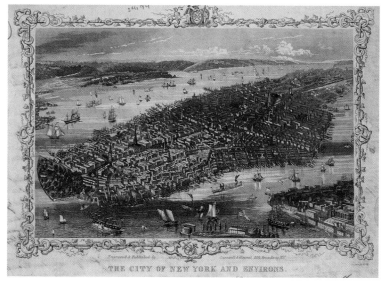

Engraving of New York City dated March 1855.
From the Collections of The Mariners' Museum.

Washington

lived with her at the time, as may an uncle, either hers or her husband's. The letters do not specify which; he is referred to throughout only as "Uncle."

By this time, recruiting had begun to slow down in New York. A few upstate regiments left the state on October 11, and one regiment raised in the city departed October 16, while another styling itself the Metropolitan Guard struggled to complete its rolls. The volunteers came nowhere near the 120,000-man quota assigned to New York, however, and on October 14 Governor Edwin Morgan ordered a draft from among the eligible men who had been enrolled in the militia. The draft was to take place on November 10, which caused some consternation among healthy New Yorkers in their twenties who, unlike George Geer, lacked a handy exemption. In the end no one was drafted, but for the whole time Geer remained at home it would have been the principal topic of discussion.[2]

Geer's letters home suggest that he departed New York around October 20, leaving Martha all his money except train fare. Despite the crowded conditions of the Allen Street apartment, he also left her fearful that she had become pregnant again. Several of Geer's letters allude to her apparent dis-

like of sex, yet he would later hint that she had played a role in the present worry.

As soon as he returned to the navy yard in Washington he began pestering every officer in his chain of command for recommendations on his appointment as a third assistant engineer. To Martha he made the oblique suggestion that if he did not get the appointment he might follow the lead of some of *Monitor*'s deck hands, who had failed to return from leave. They were simply being dropped from the ship's muster roll, and rather than go to sea for two more years at thirty dollars a month Geer thought he might find a better place aboard a civilian steamer. That job might have required some recommendations that a deserter could not easily provide, and he appears not to have worked out those details, but his first letter to Martha suggests that he was suffering from the heightened homesickness of the man who has recently tasted the tea at his own hearth.

"It was very hard when I got back here not to have any money to buy soft Bread," he wrote on October 25, "and to have to eat these hard Crackers when all the rest (or a part of them, as I was not the only one that was broke) eating Soft bread, but we have had fresh Beef every day, so I get along, but

I hope I will not have to go to sea again as a fireman and I have about made up my mind not to. If I do not get my appointment I think I shall try and get on Some Tug here, as they are not going to look after those who have run away and I have no notion of serving two Years longer."

The *Monitor* still lay in the ways at the yard, where her engines had been overhauled and new ventilation had been installed belowdecks. Carpenters had widened out the berth deck as well, taking the space from storerooms along the sides of the ship; they fashioned more storage room beneath the floor of the berth deck, which they raised high enough that the taller men needed to stoop. The crew did not board the vessel immediately, sleeping instead aboard the idle *King Philip*, and they idled away their days. Geer spent his time roaming the yard to see the sights, including test firing of the new fifteen-inch Dahlgren guns with which the next generation of monitors would be equipped. One day he wandered over to the camp of the 15th New York Engineers, to see his friend Captain Joseph Wood. But Geer seems to have easily taken offense, and his account of their meeting in his letter of October 25 suggests that Wood had somehow injured Geer's sensibilities.

U.S. Steamer Monitor
Washington Navy Yard Oct 25 [1862]

Dear Wife

Your good long Lettor came to hand yesterday. I have not sent you the Paper becaus I am out of Stamps. As soon as our Paymaster comes back I will get some money from him and then I will send the Paper. I have not been out of the Navy Yard sence I arived except once, and that was to see Jos. Wood. I promised to go and see him again but shall not, as he acted as though he did not like my Saylor Cloaths, so I shall not bother him again. . . .

I have not accomplished much with my affairs, as I have been waiting for Bankhead to return. He came yesterday, but did not come on this Vessel. He only came in the Yard, but the first Leftenant Mr. Green told me to give him my Papers tomorrow morning and he would see the Captain Signed them. He gave me an exilent recomendation, signed by him and Mr. Fly [*Acting Volunteer Lieutenant William Flye*]. I have written to Mr. Campbell to send me a recomendation, as he is sick and will not come on for some time yet.

The Monitor is out of Water yet, but they are getting ready to let her off the ways now, and probaly before I get through with this lettor she will be in the Water. It will take some time yet to finnish her, brobaly two or three weeks yet. Our men have not all got back yet; there is 10 or 11 Short, but I do not think they will come back. I suppose most of them have gon in the Armey, as the bounties are high.

I have very little news to write. I spend my time around the Yard, looking at the sights and hearing them fire that 15 in. Gun. It makes every thing shake, I can tell you, and they are only firing it with about ½ the usual charge. It must make things shake when they put in a full charge. . . .

Your husband
<u>George</u>

The delay at Washington worked to Geer's benefit, for it allowed the *Monitor*'s officers time to polish their prose endorsing his promotion. The navy yard also lay within an easy jaunt of all the government officials who stood between Geer and an officer's cap.

U.S. Str. Monitor
Washington Navy Yard Oct 29 [1862]

Dear Wife
Your welcom Lettor came to hand this morning. I am glad to hear you are all well. I have had much bettor luck than I expected. The Capt. came back and made my papers all right, and much to my surprise Mr. Campbell came back yesterday and gave me a good lettor of recomendation, and this morning Mr. Green took my Papers and had the Comodore sign then [*them*] and the Comodore sent them up to Mr. Wells, the Secretary of the Navy. So I shall probaly hear from

them in the corse of one Week. If not, Mr. Green says for me to go up and see Mr. Wells. So every thing is working nicely so far.

I cannot write you a long lettor on Wednesday as we are to busy, but will try on Sunday to write you a good one.

Yours in Haste
George

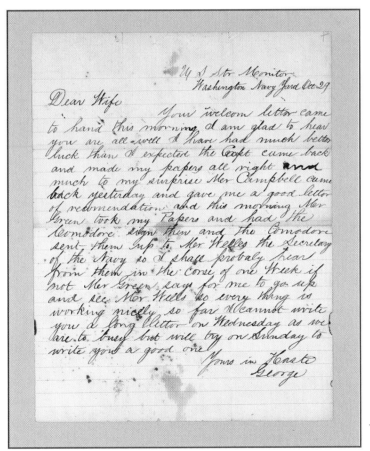

Letter from George Geer to Martha Geer, October 29, 1862, written while the Monitor *was at the Washington Navy Yard for overhaul.*
From the Collections of The Mariners' Museum.

In a few days Geer would find himself on the defensive: Martha Geer had rebuked her husband for even considering desertion—an intent he now vehemently denied.

Dear Wife

. . . You take me to task very severly at what I said about leving the vesil, but you know very well I would do no such thing. I was a little out of sorts when I wrote it, and some home Sick.

I wrote you in my last that my papers had gon in, but much to my disapointment Mr. Green told me he had forgotten them, and left them in his room until Friday. But know *[now]* I know they are in, and he said if I did not hear from them in time he would go up with me and see Mr. Wells. But I think the Monitor will not get away from here for 10 or 12 days yet, so I have plenty of time.

. . . There was a Draft of 210 Saylors arived here this morning from New York. They are for general use—some of them I suppose will go on us, as ten of our men have not come back yet.

They are fixing the Monitor up much bettor than she was before. They will make a perfect little Pallace of her. The workmen work nights and Sundays. I can hear them hammering away as I am writting. They have named her Guns Worden and Ericsson, and have the names engraved on them in very large Lettors, and also have engraved over every shot mark where it come from, so People do not have to ask so many Questions.

I went yesterday to look in my Store room for some small Tools I had in one of the Drawers and found the Workmen had stolen every one of them. When I came back I found her Penant fast to the Flag Staf, laying on the Deck, so I took it off and put it in my bag, so you see I have one of the Monitor Battle Flags. I shall send it to Gilbert. If I get my apointment I have a chance to get from one of the Workmen in the Yard an American Flag 20 ft. long, and I shall get it, I think. I suppose it is worth $25 or 30. . . .

Your Loving
George

The *Monitor* pennant Geer found, and the large American flag he may have purchased from the yard, may have contributed to a legend that arose decades later, in which Geer is supposed to have wrapped the flag of the sinking ironclad around his body before leaping to a lifeboat. In the letters he would eventually write home about the foundering of the *Monitor* Geer never mentioned performing such a patriotic gesture, but Troy's soon-to-be-elected congressman, John Griswold, bequeathed his family a flag that was supposed to have been brought to him from the *Monitor* by Geer. That flag was later donated to the Smithsonian Institution, along with the dubious tale of its rescue by Geer.[3]

George Geer used his last days in Washington to further his ambitions for promotion, dropping in on no less a personage than the nation's first assistant secretary of the navy. The efforts he described in his letters illustrate what were then the accepted means of advancing oneself in the government and military: connections and persistence. His and his brother's acquaintance with their district congressmen, his friends among the officers, and his readiness to promote his own case all proved as important as his experience to his ultimate success in an organization that was inundated with demands for appointments.

U.S. Steamer Monitor
Washington Navy Yard Nov 7 [1862]

Dear Wife

We are on board the Monitor living again and I find it cool enough for me to write in my store room. . . .

. . . I called on Mr. Fox on Thursday and he sent me to the Engineering department to get my Papers, but I had to wate so long before I had a chance to see Mr. Fox that the Clerk in the Engineering department had gon home (I mean the Clerk that had charge of the aplications as there is some 100 or more diferant Clerks). So I had no way but to go up this morning again, and after considerable running from one Room to another I at last found them and got them through as far as I could: that is, got them past and am now wating for an appointment. They told me the department never appointed acting Engineers only as they wanted them, so I will stand a chance to get my appointment as soon as they are in want of a third assistant, which may be in three days and not in three months, as there is a lot of aplications and they are taken in no order, but he put my Papers on the top of the Pile.

I believe I have not written you any thing about the improvements they have been making on the Monitor. They have torn down the Store Rooms and made the berth Deck 8 ft larger, and rased the Floor so as to make store room under it, which is an improvement. They have also put a Blower and Engine for the berth Deck to ventelate it and the Ward Room, which will be of very little use to us this Winter but next summer will be very nice, as it is as large as both of our other ones togather and blows such a blast it would nock one down. They have given the Engine a thorough repairing, and it works first rate now.

. . . It commenced to snow this morning, and the Snow fell about two inches deep, but will be all gon by tomorrow morning.

With what men have been discharged and what forgot to come back leves us twelve men short, and we have in place of them thirteen landsmen, or green hands such as I was Eight months ago, but I am glad to say most of them are Americans as far as I can judge. . . .

Your loving

George

The early snow that Geer recorded on November 7 was rare in the nation's capital. The same blizzard inundated the village of Rectortown, Virginia, less than fifty air miles to the west from the anchored *Monitor*, where that night a staff officer presented George McClellan with the orders that effectively ended his military career. The rapid, resounding victory George Geer had hoped for from this general would never come: McClellan would head back to Washington in a few days, the Army of the Potomac would go under the command of Ambrose Burnside, and the Civil War would drag on for another two and a half years.

⸱

Suddenly there was feverish activity in the navy yard, aimed at completing the *Monitor*'s repairs. Floating through Washington was a rumor that the newest Confederate ironclad was making its way down the James River. The night of November 7 the *Monitor* crew slept aboard their craft, though many of the officers would not return until the next day. At noon on November 8, the fabled ironclad backed away from its mooring and started down the Potomac—not towed this time, but proudly under its own power. When the Confederate ram failed to appear, the *Monitor* made a leisurely cruise downriver and into a placid Chesapeake Bay. Hampton Roads opened before the pilot at noon on

November 10, and he turned the wheel toward the point at Newport News where the ship had spent September.[4]

At this anchorage Geer received a small bit of welcome news: his furlough had not produced a pregnant wife.

"I got your Lettor on Saturday before we left, and I can assure you I was glad that old friend of yours has given you a call," Geer wrote her. "Not that I had any doubt that she would come, but that I know it is a very great relief to you, and you will be safe from any danger in the future as I shall not take your _advise_ again."

What Martha's "advise" with regard to sexual intimacy might have been, we can only guess. But Geer's comment suggests that she took an active role in the couple's intimate decision making. Beyond the stereotypical Victorian dictum against enjoying lovemaking, in the 1860s women had well-grounded fears associated with pregnancy. It was an era when antiseptic medicine was little understood and many women still died in or shortly after childbirth. Geer's reference to placing his wife in danger suggests one reason why husbands wished to be near their wives during confinement and delivery; for the mother, her health and the additional work and responsibility of raising another child would have caused genuine anxiety.

As it was, with her husband's departure Martha Geer once again had sole responsibility for two children. She now took some of the money Geer had left with her and went shopping—spending a grand total of six dollars. To the financially pinched Geers, it was a large sum. Geer clearly worried about how much money his wife spent; his letters include frequent references to how, in his opinion, she should make economies. Isolated as he was from his household, and a man disposed to tote up every penny, the lack of direct control over the family finances must have made him nervous, even while Martha did her best to satisfy her husband's high standards of frugality.

WASHINGTON

Dear Wife

. . . We had a very pleasant time coming down. The Chesepeak was as pleasant and Smooth as a lake, and our engines worked beautifull. I was Engineer of the new Blower Engine, and it kept me very busy, I can tell you. In fact, I have been on the jump ever sense we commenced to get ready.

I got your Lettor on Saturday before we left, and I can assure you I was glad that old friend of yours has given you a call. Not that I had any doubt that she would come, but that I know it is a very great relief to you, and you will be safe from any danger in the future as I shall not take your <u>advise</u> again.

You say you have spent $6 of your money. I don't see hardly how you are going to live through the month with your family, but I will try and draw some money and send [it]. Mind, I don't say I will, but I will try.

These new men we have are [the] damdest lazyest set of Hoggs I ever saw, and out of 13 there is but two Saylors. The rest of them never were on Salt Water before. We had to mess any way for a few days, and there was six of them in my mess, and I could hardly get any thing to eat, they were such Hoggs.

— NOVEMBER 11, 1862

. . . I did not write you in my last that I had made a Hall *[haul]* amongst the things left behind by those who <u>forgot</u> to come back. I got out of one of their Hammocks a Pair of Blankets as good as new, and exacly what I wanted and would have had to pay the Paymaster Six Dollars for as soon as it come cold. I also got two White Shirts and a pair of Pants such as Saylors ware. They will do to cut up and make Willey Summer Cloathing, although they are Stout, heavy Duck.

I also slep on the Monitor the night I wrote you, and that day we had been mooving the Stores from the King Philip, the Steamer we had been living on. The Purcer did not lock the Rooms, so I had a Pail about as large as the one you have Shugar in, so I filled that with Shugar and took 6 Papers of Coffee, one pound in each Paper, and stowed them away in my Store Room. . . . So we have a Pot of Coffee very often in the Fire Room and we do make it bully. I have some on the

Stove, and shall try a Pot as soon as I have this Lettor done.

   . . . These new men we have are [the] damdest lazyest set of Hoggs I ever saw, and out of 13 there is but two Saylors. The rest of them never were on Salt Water before. We had to mess any way for a fiew days, and there was six of them in my mess, and I could hardly get any thing to eat, they were such Hoggs. But Mr. Green . . . put all the Fire Men in a mess by them selves, so we are all old hands and every thing goes smoothly. We have three Rations stoped in the mess, which is 22.50 pr month, and that will most keep us in Potatoes and Onions, so we will pass a very pleasant Winter, I hope.

   . . . It is most Hammock time, so I will close with much love.

Your Husband
<u>George</u>

I was glad that old friend of yours had given you a call not that I had any doubt but she would come but that I know it is a very great relief to you and you will be safe from any danger in future as I shall not take your advise again You say you have spent $6 out of your money I dont see hardly how you are going to live through the month with your family but I will try and draw some money and send mind I dont say I will but I will try That Cloth you bought for Willey is very nice and I would like very much to take the little fellow out walking with his nice Clouths on but that will not be in some time I did not write you in my last that I had made a Hull amongst the things left behind by those who forgot to come back I got out of one of theirs Hammocks a Pair of Blankets as good as new and exacly what I wanted and would have had to pay the Paymaster Six Dollars for as soon as it come told I also got two White Shirts and a pair of Pants such as Saylors ware they will do to cut up and make Willey Summer Cloathing although

George Geer's letters reveal a good deal about his generation's attitudes toward personal cleanliness. In the one he penned on November 16, without a hint of embarrassment he admitted wearing a single pair of underwear for nearly three weeks—suggesting to his wife that they were so filthy when he finally peeled them off, they might do well to be boiled! References to Martha's blackened teeth suggest that Geer discerned a difference between his own casual attitude toward bathing and laundry and the potentially serious health (and cosmetic) effects of dental inattention.

U.S. Steamer Monitor
Hampton Roads Nov 16

Dear Martha

. . . I have been busy early and late sence I wrote you last, Painting, and I suppose I have any quantity of it to do. The Captain is much stricter than he was before. He has all hands Muster every morning at 9 Oclock in clean blue working Cloaths, but I am excused from muster and it saves me a great deel of washing and dressing.

That reminds me that the underclothing you washed for me I did not take off untill we arrived here, so you can imagin how I am to get them clean. I wonder if I could send them to you in a Paper and you could give them a boiling, as they require it very much. I think if I can not send them to you I will have to pay a Counterband we have to wash them for me, as there is nothing I dislike so much as Washing.

You say in your Lettor something about the 290. You need have no fear of her, as she is only a Wooden Vessel and she will never come near the Forts around New York. I think her race is most run; it will not be very long before some of our Crusers will fall in with her and put a stop to her pranks.

. . . We have three Americans in the Engineroom besides myself, so I can chum with them in place of these dand foreners. . . .

You did not think to show me when I was home where you had that Tooth out, but never mind. Give them <u>a good cleaning every morning.</u> Get that nasty black off of them, or I *[will]* write you in eve*[r]*y Lettor to Clean them. . . . Tell Willey I cannot come and fix his swing, but when I come home I will make him a new one. . . .

Your loving

<u>George</u>

For her part, Martha had evidently been reading provocative news of the "290"—the Confederate cruiser *Alabama*—and writing of the reports to her husband. A bark-rigged steamer mounting eight guns, the *Alabama* had sailed since early September in a broad arc from the Azores to the Atlantic coast, swinging fairly close to New York before turning south. Charged with destroying Northern commerce, and thus quelling United States shippers' enthusiasm for the war against the South, the *Alabama* left a wake of burning whalers and merchant-men. Though her captain had no intention of engaging any Union ironclad, the paths of the two ships would never intersect anyway: by the time Geer replied to his wife's questions about the Southern cruiser, the helmsman of that infamous ship was holding a course for the Dominican Passage and the Caribbean.

As they waited at Newport News the crew of the *Monitor* pondered their next destination. The James River seemed an unlikely assignment in winter, and the prevailing rumors seemed to hint at Charleston. Save for army incursions on the outlying islands the previous spring and summer, that city had been virtually ignored since the capture of Fort Sumter and its symbolic value demanded some action against it. Hence the Navy Department was working on an ambitious plan that required as many heavy ironclads as could be gathered. Other projects would distract official naval attention before that armada could be assembled, but at this stage the birthplace of secession seemed a good bet.[5]

George Geer's principal concern through November remained his prospects for promotion. With his ship back within range of the enemy he had lost his best opportunity for desertion, if he ever really contemplated it, and without an engineer yeoman's appointment he faced the depressing likelihood of serving an-

Lithograph depicting the Confederate steam frigate Alabama, *by Gustav W. Seitz.*
From the Collections of The Mariners' Museum.

other twenty-seven months on the meager pay of an enlisted man. Even that money came with frustrating difficulty, as Geer described in a letter that accused Paymaster Keeler of neglecting his duties. Keeler's own letters home do suggest that he spent a lot of time sightseeing, but in early December the paymaster complained to his wife of the same burden that he gave the men as an excuse for postponing their pay. In truth, the transfer of officers, the desertion of former crewmen and the addition of new ones, quarterly returns, and the storage of another cruise's provisions had all created a blizzard of paperwork for the *Monitor*'s purser.[6]

By this time, however, George and Martha Geer likely were used to coping with delays in navy pay procedures, and both of them clearly were interested in a larger issue that must have consumed many a conversation in the North—the identity and intentions of whoever was in charge of the Union army. As Geer would write on November 19, evidently in response to a comment in one of Martha's letters, he shared his officers' good opinion of George McClellan, who had just been re-lieved of his command. Like much of the *Monitor*'s crew, Geer leaned to the conservative side and scorned the increasing pressure to trans-form a war to save the Union into a crusade against slavery; he wished McClellan's replacement to favor the same political goals. *Not* accept-able to conservatives was John C. Frémont, who had come to represent the abolition faction in the army because of a proclamation he issued while commanding the Western Department in 1861. Like McClellan, he had subsequently been sent home to await orders. Geer's specula-tion about Frémont suggests that even a lowly *Monitor* sailor was thinking enough about the conduct of the war to suspect that Am-brose Burnside was merely a temporary replacement for McClellan.

U.S. Steamer Monitor
New Port News Nov 19 62

Dear Wife

Wednesday again, and again I start a Lettor to you, my Loving Matty. I have been very contented sence I have been down here, partly becaus I was busy and partly becaus I was hoping to hear from Washington. But as time slips by hope gradualy leves me and I stop expecting, although I have no particular reasons to as we have not been here two weaks yet, and still it appears as though we had not been away from here. But I suppose I am a leetle down Hearted to day. Perhaps I shall feel in bettor spirrits the next time I write.

. . . As regards money, I asked for some and the Paymaster told me he had orders from the Captain to pay all hands some money as soon as he had time, but he is very busy and would be for a fiew days yet, but he would give us money as soon as he could. My opinion is that I will get some money the first of the month, and not before, as he is a lazy old cus and is always behindhand. It is customary to sign Quaterly accounts every three months. We should have signed them the first of October and here it is most the first of December, and his excuse is that the

The Monitor *Chronicles*

210

accounts are not written up: he has not had time. So you see, that is a specimen of the man.

. . . You say it is cold and looks like Snow. I most wish I could say the same here, but I cannot, as it is uncumfortable warm. The only cold I have seen was when we ware at Washington, and there I most froze with my one Blanket. I dont see how the Soldiers stand it, with only one Blanket and no Hammock to sleep in. It must be very hard some times, but I suppose they get used to it.

I have been talking to the Docters Stewart [steward] sense I commenced this Letter. He is a stranger to me, and asked me if my name was Geer. He told me he was in the Docters Room yesterday and he hird some conversation in the Wardroom regarding me. He said it was not designed for him to hear, and he would not tell me what it was, but that I was all right, and from the conversation he should say I would soon get promoted. I think, but do not know for shure, that the Captain and Mr. Campbell have written to the department recomending my immediate promotion. It was hinted to me by one of the Engineers some days sence that something was going on I would hear from.

. . . I wish very much you could spare the money to send me one ounce of Black Silk. . . . If you can and will send it, dont get that Twist but get pretty coarse Sewing Silk, or you mint [might] get part of each. . . .

As regards McClellans removal I can form no opinion, becaus I do not know what reason the Administration had for remooving him. I have no doubt they had a good one, and the moove I hope will be for the best. I am satisfide as long as they do not appoint Fremont in his place. When they do that I shall make up my mind it is an Abolition War.

. . . With much love I am, as ever,

Your
Your
<u>George</u>

Discouraged about his chances for promotion, Geere began casting about for some other way to improve his fortune. There was always his shipboard retailing to fall back upon, and he attended to that for the pennies in profit it afforded him, but with confidence in his experience as a steam engineer he began looking beyond a government appointment to opportunities abroad.

U.S. Steamer Monitor
Newport News Nov 29 1862

Dear Wife

Your welcom Lettor came to hand to day. You say you would box my Ears for me if you was near me, for writting you such a Lettor. I only wish you was near enough; I would let you box them as much as you like, to get so clost to you.

    I . . . have been out Oystering once sence I wrote you last. . . . I took a box full, and when I had them open there was very near one Quart. I made them in a stew for my Breakfast yesterday morning, and I can tell you it was bully, and there was no want of Oysters in it. We have a way of cooking them here diferant from any you ever done. We take and put them in a box with holes bored in the bottom and put the box over a

You may say that my Guatimala skeam is another of his Castle building ideas, but you must consider that I am getting along in life and as yet have nothing ahead. Now, wile I am here, I have plenty of time to look around me and form some plans for the future. . . . I am determined, before I leve this Navy, to have some definite ideas for the future and try and follow them.

— NOVEMBER 29, 1862

The Monitor *Chronicles*

steam pipe and let them Steam until they open, and I can tell you they are lucious to put them in Butter and gullup them down. I can put away about two dozen any time. . . .

I think I will answer that Lettor I got from Albert Hicks in answer to the one I wrote to E. A. Crosby, the American Mi[ni]ster at Guatimala. I wish you would enquire at the PO what the postage is. I see in the Papers very often accounts from there and see that they are going in to the cultivation of Shugar as well as Coffee. Where they rase Shugar they must have Steam

Lithograph of the monitor-class USS Passaic, ca.1862, by Endicott & Co., Lithographers. The Passaic *continued to serve after the Civil War, ending her days as a vessel of the Georgia Naval Militia, which operated her from 1896 to 1898.* From the Collections of The Mariners' Museum.

Machinery, and they pay very large prices for Engineers in all those places or Countries, so I mint [might] find it in my intrest to take a trip down there after I get clear of the Navy. . . . You may say that my Guatimala skeam is another of his Castle building ideas, but you must consider that I am getting along in life and as yet have nothing ahead. Now, wile I am here, I have plenty of time to look around me and form some plans for the future. I have often had good ideas, but they always wanted money to cary them out, and as I never had any trade of coarse I could do only what chance threw in my way, but now I have a good trade, or profession, which will give me imployment most any whare, and especialy in new countries where Steam has not been generally introduced and Engineers are scarce and command very high Wages. And such a place I think Guatimala is. I do not say I am going there. . . . I am determined, before I leve this Navy, to have some definite ideas for the future and try and follow them. . . .

> Your Loving
> George

As December opened, the *Monitor's* life was nearly over—though no one aboard her could have guessed it at the time. Meanwhile, George Geer continued to record and comment on developments that might affect the length and outcome of the war. One of these was the launch of the USS *Passaic*, a monitor-class vessel armed with an eleven-inch Dahlgren gun and one of the big new fifteen-inch guns. She would become part of the flotilla bound for Charleston and a duel with Fort Sumter. To Geer, however, marooned on the little "cheesebox on a raft" whose war effort had been mostly symbolic, the bloody conflict of the Civil War had begun to seem remote.

"... I begin to believe there is no War," he wrote on December 3. "We lay here so peasfuly day after day, and seldom hear a Gun unless we or some of the Vessels in the Fleet fire one for practise. But I suppose we will have some of it yet, before the War is over. The Pacaic did not have very good luck coming out, as she burst her Boilers, but only slitely, and she has gon to Washington for repairs, which it will take but very fiew days to do. . . ."

More diverting was the ever-present speculation about Union military strategy, and the antics of the controversial and combative General Michael Corcoran, an immigrant Irish patriot who had commanded the 69th New York at the beginning of the war and had been appointed a brigadier after raising four new infantry regiments among New York's Irish population.

"... I was on Shore Sunday and had a run around Cochran['s] Brigade and saw him review them," he told Martha. "They are a very poorly drilled croud yet, but they will make good soldiers when they are under thorough disaplin. . . . I see by the Papers Brunside has come to a halt. I am very doubtful about his taking Richmond this Fall, or in fact ever, unless an Army march up the River under cover of the Gun Boats."

At home, though, events were occurring that would help reshape Geer's career and finally give him the opportunity for advancement he had so diligently pursued since the day he had stepped aboard the *Monitor*.

"I got a Lettor from Gilbert this week," Geer told Martha. "He . . . says Mr. Griswold has been elected to Congress and if I do not get my appointment he will get it through him. I tell you, Gilbert is a good Brother to me. He does not give up becaus he does not get me apointed the first time.

"I have jest had a call that I was wanted in the Galley by the Cook. . . . what was my surprise to have him give me a large Peach pie, which I shall prosede to devour in the most aproved fashion as soon as I finish this Lettor. . . . "

The election of John Griswold moved George Geer much closer to his coveted appointment. Griswold had been personally involved in the construction of the *Monitor*, and took a paternal interest in the ship and its crew. As a resident of Troy and a friend of the Geer family, he would be more inclined than his predecessor to further Geer's application, and indeed within days after Griswold's inauguration the Navy Department offered Geer a commission. There remained but one drama to act out aboard the *Monitor*, however, and Geer would play a crucial role.

WASHINGTON

Dear Wife

to hand this morning I am
you are all well I have had
luck than I expected the [tide]
and made my papers all right
much to my surprise the [General]
back yesterday and gave me a
recommendation and this mor[ning]
[General] took my Papers and ha[s]
Commodore sign them again...

as quick as we did
heavy Cannonading
Yorktown the
Battle going
Rachel has
and I hope
that will
untill sh
go off

warm
to it
not mu
Roads
friendly
the last
her and
Kills the
Husband
Mary
nuisance
to

Nine

THE CAROLINA SHORE

DECEMBER OF 1862 OFFERED LITTLE but discouragement
to the Union cause. The Army of the Potomac suffered a stunning set-
back at Fredericksburg on December 13 when, after struggling to secure
a foothold on the right bank of the Rappahannock, Ambrose Burnside
watched nearly thirteen thousand of his men shot down in desperate
efforts to turn both flanks of Lee's well-positioned army. Two days later
the battered Union army gave up its bridgeheads on the opposite bank
and withdrew to a dismal winter encampment, where morale began to
plummet and desertion soared.

The defeat disheartened even those Democrats like George Geer,
for whom the looming new year brought the specter of abolitionism to
their war. If the insurgent states had not been convinced to end their
resistance by the first day of 1863, President Lincoln's Emancipation
Proclamation would theoretically free all slaves in the rebellious dis-

tricts: anyone who fought for the Union after that date would thus become agents of abolition regardless of whether they wished to be. Geer doubted the wisdom of emancipation, and in light of his observations of the slaves he had seen, he clearly scorned the sentiment behind it. The week after Fredericksburg, he was not the only man in a blue uniform to entertain thoughts of abandoning the war and letting the South go its own way.

"Tell you the truth," he confessed to Martha, "I am getting half Sesesh. I am satisfide we are only wasting life and property for nothing. We will have to declair their independance, I am affrade, after all. In fact, I think after the length of time they have held their own they are entitled to their independance. I hardly know what to think of Brunside's moove. . . ."

Undercurrents of frustration and worry permeate this letter. Responding to Martha's apparent dismay over another pregnancy among their married friends renewed her husband's allusions to her part in their own close call in October, to which he added the promise, or threat, that he would terminate their marital relations. And, as though the idea of abstinence had provoked thoughts of infidelity in a serviceman's wife, he offered his violent opinion on an infamous case of a man who had usurped the affections of a married woman.

". . . You say Charles is real mean to be so careless; perhaps Julia likes such things much bettor than you do, and it may be somewhat difficult to get out at exactly the nick of time. It mint [might] be her fault, as well as his. But I think the best way for me to do is to <u>let it alone entirely</u> when I come home, so you may give up entirely <u>expecting any when I come home</u>. I am sorry <u>for you,</u> but it cannot be helped. . . ."

"I think that Sims, the seducer of Mrs. Anderson, should be linched or have his Stones and Penis cut off so he could do no more injury. I think he is the develishist vilin I ever read of."

Geer also had another, serious worry. Scarlet fever was striking the children of New York City, a dismal reality of life in an age of virulent disease. The most he could do was urge his wife to attend closely to their children in order to avoid excessive guilt if one of them should perish.

"I am sorry to hear that the Scarlot Feaver is around. Use all the precaution you can to keep the Children from getting it, so if you was to loose one of them you could not blame your self," he wrote.

Reading it today, the admonition seems curiously casual. Yet most parents of their generation expected to bury at least one child, as would Geer and Martha in years to come.

As he wrote this letter, it was December 17, just a week before Christmas. Geer guessed that his ship was destined to stay at Newport News, conjecture that indicates that naval scuttlebutt wasn't making the rounds as efficiently as usual. Rumors of a move on Charleston had subsided, but the commander of the North Atlantic Blockading Squadron, Acting Rear Admiral Samuel P. Lee, had begun planning an attack on the port of Wilmington, North Carolina, which required powerful ships of shallow draft. That called for the *Monitor* and others of her class, and within a week Geer would be writing from Hampton Roads, where the ironclad would prepare for sea.[1]

> To day I am shipped ten months. Only 60 days more and I have been in the Navy one Year. It does not seam so very long, to look back, and yet it seams a long time I have been away from you. I should feel very sad if I thought I would have to be ten months longer here, but I hope and pray this war may be ended very soon, some way.
>
> — DECEMBER 17, 1862

Dear Wife

Your kind and ever welcom Lettor togather with the bundle of Papers, Silk, and Masonic Skirt Stud all came safely to hand, and what a treat of reading matter. It will last me several days. . . .

We are Coaling Ship to day, a job we would have done on Monday but it blew a gale from the NE and the sea roled over us and did not abate until this morning.

. . . You say you are glad I am not with Brunsid. I am sorry; I only wish there was water enough in the Rapihamock to let the Monitor go up there, and we would see who would have the best of it then. I don't think they would drive our army far if they were under our guns.

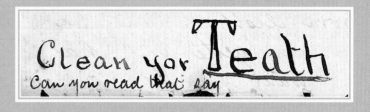

Tell you the truth, I am getting half Sesesh. I am satisfide we are only wasting life and property for nothing. We will have to declair their independance, I am affrade, after all. In fact, I think after the length of time they have held their own they are entitled to their independance. I hardly know what to think of Brunside's moove. . . .

I hear nothing more about our going from here, and I think probaly it is very doubtfull if we leve here for the presant, at any rate. I think it will depend some on what luck Brunside has.

. . . To day I am shipped ten months. Only 60 days more and I have been in the Navy one Year. It does not seam so very long, to look back, and yet it seams a long time I have been away from you. I should feel very sad if I thought I would have to be ten months longer here, but I hope and pray this war may be ended very soon, some way. . . .

Your Loving
<u>George</u>

Clean your <u>Teath</u>

Can you read that, say?

At last, on Christmas Eve, the *Monitor's* engineers called for steam and chugged over to their first anchorage in Virginia, in the middle of Hampton Roads. Alongside lay the sidewheel steamer *Rhode Island*. That same day Admiral Lee ordered Commander Bankhead to toss a hawser over to the *Rhode Island* and prepare for another long-distance tow through the open sea.[2]

The next (and last) surviving Geer letter from the *Monitor,* written on December 28, noted that Geer had endured a disappointing Christmas dinner at the hands of the ship's cook.

"As regards my Christmass, I worked all day long," he reported. "We had a Dinner that cost us about $100 each. We had every thing to make a splendid Dinner in your hands, but our Saylor Cook made very bad work cooking to suit me, but these poor devils that never had as good before thought every thing splendid."

The officers fared better, however, under the culinary attention of a new wardroom cook and his steward—Geer's friend Daniel Moore—who provided them with a variety of soups, fish, poultry and other meats, fruits, nuts, pies, and cakes. No grog graced the crew's supper, but the wardroom table glistened with goblets of cider and wine.

And while the officers took three hours for their meal, the men rushed through theirs and returned to preparations for sea.[3]

Two weeks hence Geer would tell his brother Gilbert that he had been entrusted with the task of making most of the deck watertight. He made inch-thick rubber gaskets for the ship's portholes, and daubed the hatches with red lead putty before sealing the covers over them. Other crewmen hammered ropes of oakum under the turret, but Geer—perhaps concerned about being blamed for the loss of his ship—later complained that the oakum was not sealed with pitch.[4]

Rain had been falling for several days, and the *Monitor's* pumps ran periodically to disgorge water that seeped into the vessel before the caulking had been completed. While inspecting one of the pumps, the acting chief engineer, Albert Campbell, managed to get a leg tangled in the piston linkage. Though he escaped any broken bones, Campbell's injury would confine him to bed for a while, and the captain sent him to a hospital ashore rather than carry a disabled officer to sea. The decision would save Campbell's life.

Meanwhile, in his final letter from the *Monitor,* George Geer awkwardly tried to console his wife over their separation.

"You say it makes you feel loansum when you go in the street and see Wives with their Husbands, happy togather," he pointed out, "but do you ever see some poor Widdow mooving along alone, and her Husband perhaps under the sod of Antetam or some other Battle field? Then you can say how much bettor off I am than her, for I can hope for my Husband to come home, and Hope, to her, is gon. She must seas [cease] to expect. You should think of those things, and then you could appreciate how much bettor off you are than many others."

With unwitting irony, Geer also predicted that he would see heavy fighting in the near future, and in his nervousness he spilled his ink bottle for the first time in the scores of letters he had written. Yet even the perceptive Geer could not have anticipated the looming crisis that would bring him to the brink of leaving his own widow on the streets of New York.

U.S. Steamer Monitor
Hampton Roads V__a__ Dec 28 1862

Dear Wife

Your Lettor was received to day, one day later than usual. I was somewhat uneasy for fear the money had not reached you, but I see by your Lettor you received it all OK, and I am as glad to know you got it as you was to get it.

You see by the heading of this Lettor we are still laying in Hampton Roads. We are ready in every respect for sea, and do not know the moment we will start. I begin to think this expedition is of more magnitude than I at first though[t]. There is a very large fleet of War Ships here going with us. The Pasaic is laying side of us, and the Montalk is expected every hour as well as the Weehawken and Patapsico, but we may not wate for the last two, but they will probaly join us on the cost.

I was saying this expedition is much larger than I expected. I think, some, we are going down to [the] Cost to capture every place not all ready in our hand. If so, I shall probaly see plenty of Fighting yet. I think that Sumpter will not last long when us three Iron Clads get up clost to it, especially when thesse two new ones with their 15 in. Guns get to hamering away at it. When we leve here I have no doubt we will attack the Fort at Wilmington NC, and from there moove on down to Charleston, and so on. It is what we should do, and there would then be no more accounts in the Papers of this and that vessel running the Blockade.

As regards my Christmass, I worked all day long. We had a Dinner that cost us about $100 each. We had every thing to make a splendid Dinner in your hands, but our Saylor Cook made very bad work cooking to suit me, but these poor devils that never had as good before thought every thing splendid.

There I was, filling my Ink bottle, and you see what I have done. No time to write this over again, and so I shall have to let it go.

But as regards Christmass, I cannot say it was a poor one as I was busy all day and had no time to enjoy my self, but if I could have only known you was having such good times it would have made mine a merry Christmass. But never mind. I hope next year we may spend our Christmass and New Years both togather, and every one hear after.

You say it makes you feel loansum when you go in the street and see Wives with their Husbands, happy togather, but do you ever see some poor Widdow mooving along alone, and her Husband perhaps under the sod of Antetam or some other Battle field? Then you can say how much bettor off I am than her, for I can hope for my Husband to come home, and Hope, to her, is gon. She must seas [cease] to expect. You should think of those things, and then you could appreciate how much bettor off you are than many others.

We are living now alltogather on what we get from Shore. That is, fresh Beef every day. The Captain will not allow our Stores to be broke into untill we leve here, so that looks as though we would not lay here many days. I suppose what we are wating for is the Montalk.

I should say it has been raining sence Friday good and hard, but it has cleared off to day very fine.

I am glad to know the Children faired so well [*during the outbreak of scarlet fever,* *he evidently means*]. I hope they may alwas be so fortunate.

. . . Mr. Campbell, our Chief Engineer, got caught in one of the small Pumping engines and got his Leg so badly brused he will be confined to his bed for some weeks. It is the greatest wonder he has not a broken Legg, but it was his own carelessness and no body is to blame.

I must stop or miss the mail.

Your Loving
George

Word of the Wilmington expedition had evidently leaked. With Pamlico Sound closed, Wilmington was the next port down the coast open for blockade runners, and it was the best in the Confederacy. Two inlets at the mouth of the Cape Fear River doubled the difficulty to Union blockaders, and Confederates had built substantial fortifications near New Inlet. As early as May 11, the day the CSS *Virginia* exploded, Gideon Welles tried to arrange for an attack on the Cape Fear defenses by the *Monitor* and a host of other Union vessels. Operations up the James River preempted that proposal, but the armies in Virginia now lay upon the Rappahannock River, where the big gunboats could not go. Major General John Foster's Union army at New Bern, North Carolina, stood ready to strike at Wilmington by land while the navy attacked up the river, and with enough ironclads there seemed to be a good chance of reducing the fortifications. At Hampton Roads there gathered at the end of December the ironclads *Monitor*, *Passaic*, and *Montauk*. Two others, the *Weehawken* and the *Patapsco* (both of which would sink at Charleston), were ordered down from Northern shipyards, but would not arrive until late January.[5]

The three ironclads already there might have offered broadsides heavy enough. One problem lingered, however. Both inlets into the

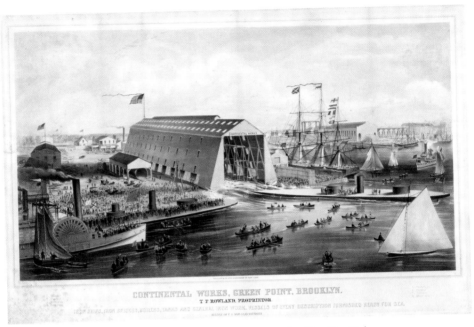

*Lithograph showing the busy Continental Iron Works in Green Point, Brooklyn, New York.
This yard built eight monitor-class ironclads for the Union navy, including the original* Monitor,
the Passaic, *and the* Montauk. *Endicott & Company, Lithographers.*

FROM THE COLLECTIONS OF THE MARINERS' MUSEUM.

Cape Fear River drew very shallow water, and naval planners wondered if even the monitors could wallow across the bars there.

Commander Bankhead, himself a Carolinian, remembered those inlets from his days on the coastal survey. He had commanded a craft there with a nine-foot draft, which could barely maneuver the New Inlet; the *Monitor* drew the least water of any of the ironclads, and he doubted that even its draft of ten feet, four inches could navigate that channel in winter. The Old Inlet, however, was a possibility, he told Admiral Lee, if no obstructions had been placed there. On the other hand, the commander of the *Passaic* gave a discouraging opinion about the Old Inlet. Accounting for two-foot swells, that officer judged that this passage had an effective draft of eleven and a half feet at high tide, while his ironclad drew about twelve feet. The *Montauk* likewise drew nearly twelve feet in fighting trim.[6]

These considerations all taken into account, the *Monitor* constituted the best hope for slipping behind the forts and striking their vulnerable side. But by the time she had been caulked and battened, another storm came up; the entire operation was postponed until she could head out. It was not until several hours after noon on December 29 that the *Rhode Island* sailed out with the little ironclad trailing by two big hawsers, heading for the expedition rendezvous at Beaufort, North Carolina. Only three hours before the *Monitor* left Hampton Roads the *Montauk* arrived, under the command of none other than John Worden. If Worden saw his old ironclad before it departed, it was for the first time since the fight with the *Virginia*, and it would be his final glimpse. That same day the *Passaic* went out under tow of the *State of Georgia*, and the army commander at Fort Monroe ordered eight thousand additional troops to General Foster.[7]

At about 6:00 P.M., the *Monitor* hit the open sea beyond Cape Henry, where for nearly twelve more hours the wind and water remained relatively calm. Then the swells increased and the unsealed oakum began washing out from beneath the turret, just enough remaining to hold the tower dangerously high above its brass bearing. Every wave washed freely onto the berth deck, soaking the crew and draining into the bilge. Later, George Geer would report that the pumps kept up with the flood throughout the day, but at evening the wind picked up and enough water washed under the turret to concern Commander Bankhead. The rising seas caused the ship to balk like a mule at her hawsers, and that eroded more of the oakum. Bankhead signaled for the *Rhode Island* to stop, so the *Monitor* could make her own headway and perhaps level off, but the prow of the ironclad only ducked into the sea when the tow cables fell slack, and as much water or more poured into the gaping fissure.

By late evening the *Monitor* was in jeopardy. The volume of water inside her hull caused the ship to pitch heavily into each sea, submerging the pilothouse and sometimes pouring into the blower pipes despite the extensions fitted at the navy yard. At every plunge the overhanging armor would strike the water hard, and all hands began to fear that the iron plating would be torn away from the wooden hull.

In an account written a fortnight later, Geer wrote that at about 9:00 P.M. he approached the watch engineer, Third Assistant Engineer Robinson Hands, and suggested that he prepare the big centrifugal pump for use, since the Worthington pump seemed to be losing against the torrent. Hands told him not to bother, said Geer, adding that Joseph Watters, a second assistant engineer who had come aboard in Campbell's place as acting chief, overrode Hands and instructed Geer to assemble the pump. Commander Bankhead, however, reported that it was he who told Watters to prepare the centrifugal pump, and Watters ordered the big pump started when the water rose more than an inch deep on the floor of the engine room. Geer, who operated the pump, said that it threw a stream of water as big around as a man's body. He felt that it stopped, or at least slowed, the increase in volume for as much as an hour. Then the water level began rising rapidly, filling the ash pits below the fires, thus cutting off the draft and reducing the heat under the boilers. The blowers that were meant to ventilate the fireboxes were taking seas through their pipes on deck, and instead of fanning the fires they began belching water into them. These accumulating difficulties cost steam

pressure, and Watters asked Bankhead for permission to slow the main engines so he could divert pressure to the pumps. But even that failed to keep up with the intake of water, leading Commander Bankhead to assume that the upper and lower hulls had finally separated; at 10:30 P.M. Bankhead sent up the distress signal he had arranged with the captain of the *Rhode Island*.[8]

Bankhead knew that his towline to the *Rhode Island* could prove their undoing, for when that ship hove to the *Monitor* might be driven into it and pierce the hull at the waterline. If that happened, everyone would drown. He sent a sailor out on the treacherous deck with an axe to cut the cables. Two decades later, Francis Butts, one of the new recruits on the *Monitor*, would recall that it was Quarter Gunner James Fenwick who made the first attempt, only to be washed overboard and lost. Boatswain's Mate John Stocking took another axe and followed Fenwick, claimed Butts, frantically severing the hawsers before he, too, was carried off by a wave. Paymaster Keeler remembered no such tragedies, instead recording that an officer cut the cable and returned safely, although everyone had expected him to be swept into the sea.[9]

Boats from the sidewheel steamer dipped

precariously into the frothing sea and made their way to the ironclad, which had dropped its anchor in an effort to come to rest. The passage took time, though, and the engineer watch remained in the engine room so long as any steam remained to work the pumps. A launch and a cutter reached the floundering *Monitor*, and Bankhead ordered as many men into them as they could hold safely; a few men were carried away as they tried to descend from the turret. The two loaded boats started back for the *Rhode Island*, which had pulled away to avoid collision, while the ironclad settled lower in the water and the sea crashed directly against the turret. Around midnight, Watters came up to report that the water had drowned all the fires and the pumps had stopped.[10]

Down in the engine room, Geer finally abandoned his stilled pump, slogging toward the turret ladder through knee-deep water. The boats had returned for more passengers, carefully approaching the submerged iron deck, and men scrambled over the edge of the turret while Commander Bankhead held the painter of one boat for them. The sea had grown even rougher, and some men who tried jumping into the boat fell instead into a watery grave. Others who tried climbing down on the deck could not

"*The Wreck of the Iron-clad 'MONITOR.'*"
Line engraving, ca. 1864. The USS Rhode Island, *which was towing the* Monitor, *is shown in the background.*
From the Collections of The Mariners' Museum.

keep their footing either, and washed over the side. Geer plunged into the water and tried to swim for a boat, but a wave washed him back across the deck. He grabbed a rope that a man beside him had missed, then splashed back into the wake of a passing wave and swam close enough for one of the oarsmen in the boat to grasp him and pull him in. Of those who fell into the water he apparently was the only one who was saved.

A few timid souls remained on the *Monitor*'s turret as the boats rowed back to the *Rhode Island*. When this second shuttle had climbed onto the *Rhode Island*, another of

I am sorry to have to write you that we have lost the Monitor.

— JANUARY 2, 1863

the boats made an attempt to save the last few men on the doomed vessel. The lantern on top of the turret twinkled out before they reached her, though, and the rescue boat overshot its mark. Before the boat's crew could turn back to the mother ship they had lost sight of her, and then themselves disappeared into the storm. Those they had meant to save went down with the ironclad.

Lantern recovered from the Monitor *wreck site.*
FROM THE COLLECTIONS OF
THE MARINERS' MUSEUM.

The next morning a schooner from Maine picked up the *Rhode Island*'s men, although it would be several days before their shipmates learned of the rescue. When the officers and men of the lost ship mustered on the deck of the *Rhode Island* that last morning of 1862, they numbered sixteen fewer than they had a day before. Four officers had been lost, including two third assistant engineers: Robinson Hands and Samuel Lewis, whom Landsman Butts claimed to have seen lying sick in his bed just before the sinking. Among the drowned was also Geer's friend Daniel Moore, the officers' steward.[11]

The *Monitor* crewmen huddled on the cold deck as best they could in their wet clothing and tried to sleep. Most, including George Geer, had lost any jackets they owned and shivered themselves to restless sleep. Lest Martha read the news of the disaster and suppose her husband among the lost, Geer borrowed a small sheet of paper, inscribed it with the wrong year, and wrote her a letter.

The Monitor *Chronicles*

U.S. Steamer Rhode Island
Jany 2 1862 [1863]

Dear Wife

I am sorry to have to write you that we have lost the Monitor, and what is worse we had 16 poor fellows drownded. I can tell you I thank God my life is spaired. Besides the 16 we lost one boat that was sent from this Steamer with 11 semen in is missing. We have crused two days for them, and have given them up for lost. I have not time to write you any more, but do not worry. I am safe and well. Write to Troy and let them know I am safe.

Your Loving
Husband
Geo S. Geer

Letter from George Geer to Martha Geer, dated January 2, 1862 [1863], from the USS Rhode Island, two days after the sinking of the Monitor at Cape Hatteras, North Carolina.

From the Collections of
The Mariners' Museum.

The sinking of the *Monitor* ended any hope of success for the Wilmington expedition, and the *Rhode Island* returned to Hampton Roads with the survivors of the famous ironclad. Those of the crew who had been with the *Monitor* since her launching were so discouraged that the enlisted men among them, including Geer, had already composed a petition for discharge when the *Rhode Island* dropped anchor in Virginia. Despairing of earning his long-aspired-for appointment as an engineer, Geer hoped to join his family at home. Commander Bankhead and Admiral Lee dutifully forwarded the petition to Washington, where it would eventually be rejected. At such a juncture in the war, the government was not inclined to release a score of experienced seamen when they might be put to good use elsewhere.[12]

> *Some of the men that we lost were the best in the Ship, and all the Officers lost were the best ones.*
>
> — JANUARY 6, 1863

Barring a discharge, Geer most wanted an assignment to another ironclad, such as the *Passaic*.

"I suppose you are like me: anctious to know what the Navy Department will do with me know [now]," he wrote Martha on January 6. "We do not any of [us] know, but probaly will before I write you again. I am in hopes that we will be sent to N York and put in one of the New Monitors. You must not think becaus we have lost the Monitor that Vessels like her cannot be built to stand, as the Pasaic was in the same gale and stood it furst rate. You need not worry for me, as I am always looking out for No. 1 and am not going to get killed or Drowned in this War."

Geer's information about the *Passaic* was as unreliable as his understanding of the loss of the *Rhode Island*'s boat crew, for the *Passaic* herself had come within an ace of sinking in the same storm that finished the *Monitor*.[13]

The *Monitor* crewmen next found themselves lodged aboard the old sailing frigate *Brandywine*. The Navy Department could not seem to determine where they should be, which also may have explained the navy's failure to issue the survivors clothing or blankets in the dead of winter. Freezing, demoralized, and in administrative limbo, Geer wrote again of deserting:

Jany 8 1863
U.S. Store Ship Brandawine
Hampton Roads Va

Dear Martha

. . . You see I date this Lettor from the Brandawine. The Road Island had to go to sea and the Admeral put us on here. There has no word come from the Navy department yet about us, and it is shamefull the way we are treated. We have had to sleep on the Deck with no bedding or blankets (unless we could borrow Coats from some of the Saylors, who have been very kind to us), and only what cloaths we had on at the time. I have not had any thing off of me sence we were saved, and not one cent of money. It was only by the hardest Begging I got this Paper and Onvelope to write you. . . . So when you write me in future send me paper, envelopes, & Stamps, and I will write you with Lead Pencil.

. . . I can tell you it is hard work sleeping on the Cold Deck and most freezing, as it is the Coldest now it has been this year. I am in hopes we will be sent on to New York

> *I could not tell you how often you and the children were on my mind that awfull night. In fact, I could think of nothing else but how you would get along if I was drowned, and I believe the Thoughts of you made me use greater exertions than I could otherways to save my self.*
>
> — JANUARY 8, 1863

and get Liberty there before we are put in any other vessel, if we are. I very much doubt their ever seeing any of us again if we once get out side of the Navy Yard Gate.

I received a Lettor from Gilbert to day. He says he is still trying to get me an apointment. . . .

. . . I am fearfull our good time of writting each other is goin for if they put us in another vessel we will probaly be put in some sea going Steamer. So you must put up with it untill I can get away from here some way, as I shall never serve my three years out and I may as well get away first as last. . . . I could not tell you how often you and the children were on my mind that awfull night. In fact, I could think of nothing else but how you would get along if I was drowned, and I believe the Thoughts of you made me use greater exertions than I could otherways to save my self.

Your

George

Geer wrote to his brother Gilbert as soon as Martha sent him paper, offering a firsthand account of the *Monitor*'s demise. Like many of the participants of memorable events in this war, he embellished his own part, but only slightly. The relatively minor exaggeration may have been intended for the eye of the New York freshman congressman Griswold, who could still be of use in forwarding the engineer's appointment Geer so fervently desired.

U.S. Store Ship Brandawine
Hampton Roads Jany 13 1863

Dear Brother

. . . I suppose you are anctious to know the particulars about our <u>little Pet.</u> I cannot attempt to give you a full description in this Lettor, but will give you what I can. We started from Hampton Roads on Monday, about 2 oclock PM in Tow of the side wheel Steamer Rhode

Island. We ware secured to her by two Hawsers, one of them about as large as your legg and the other very little smaller. I was told by Mr. Green, the first Left [*first lieutanant*], and the Chie[*f*] Engineer to put the Hatches on, and if poseable get them tight. I put them on with Red Lead putty, and and [sic] the Port Holes I made Rubber Gaskets one inch thick and in fact had every thing about the ship in the way of an opening water tight. Around and under the Tower the Captain had Oakum put, but did not put any Pitch over it and the sea soon washed the Oakum out and the Water came under the Tower and down on the Berth Deck in Torents. But our pumps were sufficent to keep the ship free without using any of the extra or large Pumps.

Every thing went along finely untill Thursday, about noon, when it commenced to Cloud up and looked as though we would have a rough time before long. Soon the sea commenced to break over us and wash up against the Tower with a fearfull rush, and the sea was white with foam, but I was satisfide she would stand it out unless the storm should increase. About 4 oclock we were in sight of Hatras Light House and I thought as soon as we got past the cape it

would clear up. But no, it commenced to blow harder, and by 6 oclock I was satisfide we could not save her, as every time she rased on a sea she would come down very heavy on her over-reaching sides and her bottom would shiver like a leaf, and I made up my mind she would not stand that long before her bottom would give away.

About 9 oclock I went to Mr. Hands, the Engineer, and asked him if I had not bettor get the Large steam Pump ready in case we should need it, but he thought we would not need it. But Mr. Waters, our Chief (who took Mr. Campbell's place when we sent him to the Hospital) stood by and herd our Conversation and told me to go and get it ready. It took 15 or 20 moments to get the Hose attached, and Waters stood by untill I had it ready to start. He then told me to take charge of it and stay by all the time if I had orders to start it. I then went and looked in the Bilge and saw she was making water faster than the Pumps on the Engine discharged it, so I went on top of the Tower and reported it to the Captain. He told me to go down and start the big Steam Pump. I done so, and the Pump threw a stream as large as your body, and for about one hour the Water did not gain. Nor did we gain on it much, but about 11

THE CAROLINA SHORE

oclock the Water rose very fast and I was satisfide it was all up with her. I staid by the Pump untill the water was up to my knees and the Cylinders to the Pumping Engines were under Water and stoped. She was so full of Water and roled and pitched so bad I was fearfull she would role under and forget to come up again. There was not over 15 of us below at this time, and I went on top of the Tower and found that the boats from the R.I. was taking us off.

I can tell you, it looked rather serious to attempt to get in the Boat, but I knew I mint [might] as well be drowned trying to reach the Boats as to go down in the Monitor, so I jumped off the Tower and made for the Boat. A wave struck me and washed me acrost the Deck. I caught the Ridge roap, but some body side of me was swep over board and drowned. I started again as soon as the Wave had passed over, and this time reached the Boat and was Saved, and I can tell you I would not like to try it over again. It is as clost as I care to [come to] risking my life.

Sence then We have been treated in the most shamefull manner. We have only what clothing we hapened to have on, and have had to sleep on the soft side of a Plank with nothing to cover us. And how long they will keep us this way we cannot tell, but it is full time they gave us Hammocks and cloathing, or discharged us.

It is useless to send me any thing untill I find out what they are going to do with me. I may be ordered on some vessel any moment. I wish if you get any answer from Senitor Harris you would write me. Give my Love to Father and Mother. I shall get the best of the Government by the Loss of our accounts about $50.

Your Brother
George

The officers of the *Monitor* had long since been paid and sent home on leave, but the enlisted men seemed to have been forgotten by the Navy Department. Secretary Welles eventually rejected their petition for discharge, instead issuing instructions to pay them one fifth of the pay due on their accounts, and to allow them two weeks' leave, but even so the survivors endured nearly four weeks of discomfort and virtual neglect at the hands of their own service.[14]

Brandywine Jany 17 1862 [1863]

Dear Wife,

Here we are still, and God only knows how long we will remain here. We have not herd one word about what is to be done with us. I am getting used to sleeping on the Deck, so my bones do not ach as bad as they did at first.

It is useless to send me much Paper at one time, as I have no place to put it, and what you sent me is stolen, so I am obliged to use part of one of your Lettors. The stamps came all right.

I am sorry to hear Willey is sick. Give my love to him and tell him I will dround that Doctor if he hurst [hurts] Willey.

. . . I am very much in hopes we will be sent on to NY before we are put in any Vessel, as I will never go in one if I once get my foot out of the Navy Yard Gate.

Your
<u>George</u>

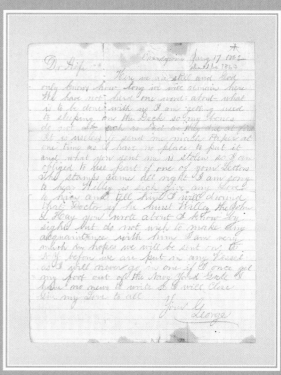

Disgusted with the treatment he and his *Monitor* shipmates endured at the hands of his own government, Geer seemed to be increasingly serious about deserting the navy. Dissatisfaction ranged beyond his neglected contingent, however, as Geer discovered from his conversations with other sailors passing time aboard the *Brandywine*. The passing of the deadline for Lincoln's Emancipation Proclamation may have fueled the disenchantment, as it did in the army, where desertion was soaring.

In what must have seemed like an unending drama of deprivation, Geer also had to worry about his family. Just as the Navy Department left him sleeping on a cold deck with no blankets for weeks at a time, it also failed to provide immediate relief for the families of sailors whose ships had been lost. Geer suddenly had to find some other source of money for his wife until his government income could be reestablished. To make matters worse, his little boys had contracted some kind of illness, so serious in Willey's case that Martha had called in a doctor. Yet, bit by bit, conditions were improving, and soon George Geer would be launched on a new phase of his navy service.

U.S. Store Ship Brandayne
Hampton Roads Jany 25 1863

Dear Wife

Sence I wrote you last we have had a change of <u>Under Clothing</u> and <u>Lice.</u> The Purcer told us he could not stand it to see us situated so any longer, so he said we mint [might] draw what we were most in want of and he would have to trust in a great degree our Honor to pay him when our accounts arived, and I can say he will not lose any thing by me, at any rate. I drew from him a Pair of Drawers, Under Shirt, & Bar of Soap. The Drawers and Undershirt are the best I ever saw in the Navy. They are Blue nitt ones, and real warm. So with the *with the Soap I had a good <u>cold</u> wash and threw my Shirt over board, <u>Lice</u> and all (<u>poor things</u>), and I can tell you I feel bettor to get clear of the <u>dear creatures</u>, for you know they are so affectionate and <u>cling so clost</u> that they made them selves in fact disagreeable to me.*

— JANUARY 25, 1863

Soap I had a good <u>cold</u> wash and threw my Shirt over board, <u>Lice</u> and all (<u>poor things</u>), and I can tell you I feel bettor to get clear of the <u>dear creatures</u>, for you know they are so affectionate and <u>cling so clost</u> that they made them selves in fact disagreeable to me. <u>Isn't that astonishing?</u> But to lay all jokes aside, I can tell you it is a relief to be free from their continual bitting and me scratching.

I think there is no use of your going after the half pay, as the Paymaster here, a very nice man, tells me that when a ship is lost it is always the custom to stop the ½ pay. But I am confident I will be able to send you money before the first. But I wish you would let me know if Rachel could lend you for, say, two weaks, if I could not get any before. If not, let me know at once and I will write to Gilbert, as he wrote as soon as he heard of the loss that if I wanted money or any thing else to write to him, but I wrote him not to send me any here as it mint [*might*] never reach me.

I herd something about us yesterday that, if true, will make both you and me glad. Perhaps in my next I may be able to tell you what it is. . . .

You, I suppose, know that this is a Receiving Ship as well as a Store Ship, and there is Crews and parts of Crews coming and going

THE CAROLINA SHORE

every day, so I have a chance of conversing with men from most of the Vessels in the Navy, and I find them all down on the War, and hardly one but would desert the first chance. So I think the leaders will have to bring the War to a close some way, or the Saylors and Soldiers will for them.

. . . I shall wate very anctiously for your Lettor to hear of the full recovery to health of those two little darlings. . . .

Your Loving
George

The "something" Geer reported in his January 25 letter was his promotion. Persistent lobbying, and possibly the loss of two third assistant engineers who perished with the *Monitor*, had finally yielded success. On January 19, 1863, an official hand registered Geer's appointment to that rank, and five days later orders made their way to Hampton Roads assigning him to the USS *Galena*, from whose decks he had seen the slaughter at Drewry's Bluff. On February 2 he wrote to Martha of having been aboard the *Galena* "ten days," which suggests that he received his new orders on or just after January 25. He doubtless reported immediately, given the miserable accommodations on the *Brandywine*, and the paymaster on his new ship would have equipped him with uniforms and bedding right away. He hesitated for several days before writing home, perhaps wishing to surprise Martha in person, but after more than a week he could wait no longer and wrote her a brief note, proudly signing it with his new title.[15]

Dear Wife

I am on board of this Vessel, where I have been for the past ten days. I have permission to go to N. York for Seven days, and have not written you as I expected to leve every day, but could not as the Paymaster did not make his appierance. He arrived here on Saturday, and told me he would be ready to pay me on Tuesday, so you can look for me on Friday or Saturday.

I am well. Love to all.

Your Husband
Geo. S. Geer
3rd Ast. Engineer,
USN

At last Geer had reached a station that would allow him to honor his contract with the navy. He had also obtained the skills and credentials he would need to begin a civilian career after the war. And although he would remain nearly three more years on the rolls of the U.S. Navy, he had at last found the opportunity for which he had enlisted at the outset.

THE CAROLINA SHORE

Dear Wife ... I received your
short Letter and it ...
a relief to me to know ...
along so finely I hope ...
new home will be a happy ...
strange it seams to me ...
ise you have moored ...
I will not go home ...
I get on shore but will go ...
along Allen st to find where ...
Wife lives. (you know ...
I get back) I will have to ...
for a lost Wife and two ...
Can any body tell me where ...
look for a very ...

as we did
Cannonading
on there must
going on up
left the
she has
be like a
gets Married
Horne while
she must
a Sunday
this Weeke is
it takes the
and make
Give my Love to
all and all
here and keep
going on
along
am extra
and tell

Ten

THE CAMPAIGN
TO RECOVER
THE *MONITOR*

ON AUGUST 25, 1999, *at 7:20 A.M., the research vessel* Cape Fear *pulled away from the dock at the Hatteras Landing Marina, carrying staff from the National Oceanic and Atmospheric Administration (NOAA) and five divers from the Florida-based Cambrian Foundation and the National Undersea Research Center associated with the University of North Carolina at Wilmington. Just two months earlier, in June, navy divers from the USS* Grasp *and Mobile Diving and Salvage Unit 2 had made thirty descents to the wreck, exploring and photographing the hull's interior, including the engine room and the galley, and recovering lead weights and a crumpled copper oil cup. This day, the last dive day for the 1999 season, dawned clear and calm; light winds and negligible swells offered perfect conditions for the day's work.*

At mid-morning two teams of divers entered the water. As they completed their 240-foot descent to the wreck, they noted with relief that there was little or no current at the bottom and visibility around the Monitor's *remains was* more than eighty feet. For the NOAA expeditions, the summer had been a mixed exercise, with some notable progress mingled with delay—dives curtailed or canceled due to strong currents, inclement weather, or both. No matter how careful the plans and dedicated the personnel, nature's whimsy ruled in the Monitor National Marine Sanctuary, just as it did the winter night when the ironclad sank.

This day, though, the excellent conditions would allow the dive teams to make the most of their short time on the wreck—a window of twenty-five minutes defined by the requirements for safe dive operations in water so deep. Team 1 was tasked with conducting a stem-to-stern video survey of the wrecked vessel, with one diver driving a scooterlike vehicle and towing a second diver who operated the video camera, making yet another of the recordings that have become crucial for keeping tabs on the wreck's status. Meanwhile, the three divers of Team 2 checked corrosion readings on the turret and armor belt and took a survey of loose objects scattered nearby. When they surfaced later that morning, they would bring back to the Cape Fear items once used by the Monitor crew, plus a series of digital photographs. With the sun now well into its transit across the sky, all that remained for them to do was to secure the precious recovered artifacts, tend to their gear, and head for home, once again leaving the Monitor to her restless solitude.

The wreck of the USS Monitor *as it lies on the sea floor sixteen miles off Cape Hatteras, North Carolina.*
COURTESY ROD FARB.

In 1973, on an August afternoon in the one hundred and eleventh year after the USS *Monitor* disappeared into churning seas off Cape Hatteras, North Carolina, remote cameras operated by two scientists—nautical archaeologist Gordon P. Watts and marine geologist John Newton—located the little armor-plated gunboat. The vessel lay sixteen miles offshore in 240 feet of water. The search for the *Monitor*'s remains had been long and frustrating, and at first the camera images were difficult to interpret. Another six months would pass before Watts realized, in a 2:00 A.M. flash of inspiration, that the murky pictures indeed showed the wreck. Pummeled by storm waves and swift ocean currents that sweep over the Eastern Continental Shelf, the ironclad had rolled during her descent, coming to her final rest on a rather flat, sandy bottom, with the upended hull's stern askew atop the famous turret. Scattered nearby were small objects that had once been accoutrements of daily life aboard the ironclad; later, four hundred feet from the sunken ship, divers would find its 1,500-pound anchor. In January 1975, the wreck of one of the world's first ironclad warships was desig-

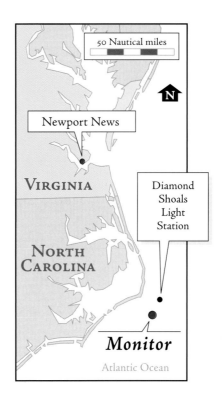

Location of the Monitor *wreck off Cape Hatteras, North Carolina.* COURTESY THE DAILY PRESS.

nated the nation's first marine sanctuary, to be administered by NOAA, the National Oceanic and Atmospheric Administration. Between 1977 and 1983 NOAA-led expeditions recovered the anchor, a brass navigation lantern, and more than one hundred other small artifacts. In 1998 a NOAA-navy expedition recovered the ship's propeller and part of its shaft, delivering it to The Mariners' Museum in Newport News, Virginia, which is Principal Museum for the *Monitor* National Marine Sanctuary.

A freshly retrieved discharge valve from the Monitor *on board the recovery ship* Kellie Chouest. *Deeply corroded, this valve is currently undergoing conservation at The Mariners' Museum.*
FROM THE COLLECTIONS OF THE MARINERS' MUSEUM.

Collapsed section of the Monitor's *hull as it appeared in 1997.*
COURTESY MONITOR NATIONAL MARINE SANCTUARY (NOAA).

Although the *Monitor* National Marine Sanctuary is but a single nautical mile in diameter, it chances to be the crossroads for two powerful ocean currents—the southerly flowing Labrador Current and the Gulf Stream, which at that point is moving to the north and east. Their interaction results in environmental conditions—weather, water temperature and turbidity, currents and sea surface characteristics—that change without warning. Time, the ocean, and bad luck have exacted such a severe toll on the remains of the ironclad that what is left of her is perilously close to disappearing forever.

Although they have been torn by currents and other mechanical stresses, the *Monitor*'s iron plates also have been giving up their substance to the sea ever since the stormy night she slipped beneath the waves. Researchers estimate that, in the warm, oxygen-rich waters off Cape Hatteras, oxidation and electrochemical corrosion have stolen as much as 90 percent of the original thickness of the ship's iron plating. What remains is breached in places by holes; except for the armor belt and turret, the *Monitor*'s once-strong iron body now is a fragile, vulnerable shell. It's impossible to accurately guess the fate of some parts of the ironclad, because during World War II, navy testing of a secret "underwater object locator" involved the use of depth charges on targets—possibly including the *Monitor*.

Remarkably after all these assaults, the ironclad's turret is more or less intact; the aft section of the lower hull, where the ship's engine, boilers, and other machinery provide support, and the aft portion of the armor belt are recognizable but seriously deteriorated. At the stern a major segment of the hull and its iron belt are missing. Farther forward, the lower hull has collapsed. The ironclad's sizable rudder, built of wood swathed with iron plating, has yet to be located, though it may lie hidden by sand somewhere in the wreck's debris field. The *Monitor's* two eleven-inch Dahlgren cannon also are nowhere to be seen; they may still be inside the turret under a blanket of silt.

The imminent loss of what some have called the most important United States Navy ship ever built has become a clarion call to action for naval historians, marine archaeologists, and for everyone across whose imagination the quirky, remarkable little *Monitor* has ever sailed. What follows here provides a glimpse of the efforts being made on her behalf.

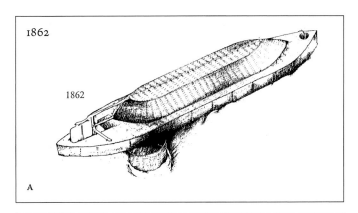

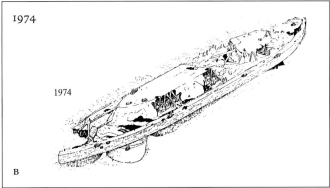

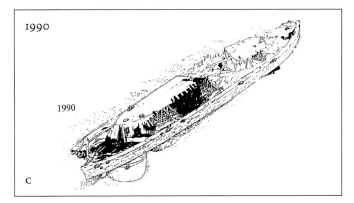

The rapidly progressing deterioration of the Monitor from 1862 to 1990 is evident in sketches B and C. Sketch A is an artist's re-creation of the position in which the Monitor came to rest on the sea floor, based on the positions of the ironclad's components as they were discovered in 1974. Courtesy of Monitor National Marine Sanctuary (NOAA).

Although various artifacts were recovered from the *Monitor* wreck site in the years immediately following its discovery, the ruined ironclad only surfaced as a candidate for a major effort in the late 1980s, when corrosion studies commissioned by NOAA reported an alarming increase in the rate at which the wreck was disintegrating. There was also clear evidence that, her status as a marine sanctuary notwithstanding, the *Monitor* was being damaged by fishing nets and boat anchors. NOAA's response to the emergency was swift and unequivocal. In the short term, the agency stepped up its efforts to track the corrosion, and today NOAA and a cadre of other players are working to improve the odds that at least some of the *Monitor* can be wrested from the sea.

Many interconnected factors are shaping their work. One is the wreck's difficult and often dangerous physical setting in deep water laced with swift currents. Another crucial concern for historians and marine archaeologists is the detailed mapping of the wreck and the surrounding area, including the nature and location of artifacts. A third core issue is the hefty price tag for the project, estimated in 1999 at $10 million for a partial recovery operation plus close to another $10 million for post-recovery conservation work. For the most part, such a sum will almost certainly have to come from federal

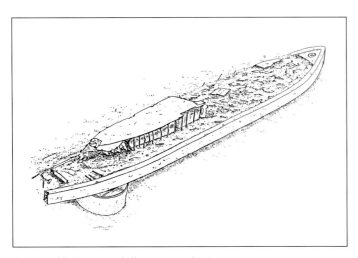

Drawing of the Monitor's hull as it appeared in June 1999.
Courtesy of Monitor National Marine Sanctuary (NOAA).

coffers, and the question of whether funding will be forthcoming remains to be resolved. Cost and other practical concerns, including the poor overall condition of the wreck, already have dictated that any recovery effort focus only on the most significant historic components, mainly the engine and turret. In the meantime, NOAA staff are making the most of available resources—especially navy divers, for whom work on the wreck provides valuable training, and divers from the Cambrian Foundation and the National Undersea Research Center.

When the USS *Monitor* was towed out of Hampton Roads on December 29, 1862, she embodied the dream of her creator John Ericsson, who hoped to build the world's first impregnable warship. She also was literally a seagoing experiment, sporting more than forty pioneering

Diver surveying a section of the Monitor's hull. This view from the stern shows the aft engine bulkhead. COURTESY ROD FARB.

THE CAMPAIGN TO RECOVER THE *MONITOR*

features, including her revolving turret, armored deck, flush toilets, and a galley situated below the waterline. Today the *Monitor* is again the subject of experimentation, this time geared toward the harsh reality of her impending demise.

If the *Monitor*'s recoverable remains are to be retrieved, only a phased strategy will make that historic rescue possible. Planning begun in the early 1990s and involving site inspections, surveys, and mapping filled in some glaring blanks in the recovery script. Much of this work, especially the detailed documentation of the wreck's condition and the precise, three-dimensional positioning of its parts, comes under the heading of marine archaeology and may complete the public history of the *Monitor*'s final refitting and her last moments as she plunged to the sea floor. Inevitably, though, this scientific work also has tracked the accelerating deterioration of the wreck as corroded parts of the iron hull collapse under stress and wooden underpinnings fall victim to external trauma, decay, and the incessant dismantling activities of marine organisms.

The *Monitor*'s hull was built with a central bulkhead dividing it midships into two main functional areas. The worst of the recent damage she has sustained has occurred in the ironclad's aft section. For instance, as recorded in NOAA's video archive of the wreck, the skeg—a long, slim structure that provided support for the propeller and the rudder—was torn away from its original position in 1991, probably by a fishing boat anchor. As the skeg was wrenched out of kilter, with it went the aft lower hull plate, which until then had protected interior structures and spaces including the engine room. Luckily, the propeller was unharmed. But NOAA documentation clearly shows the serious deterioration that has occurred in the years since Gordon Watts first peered at fuzzy images of the wreck. A full six-foot section of the aft armor belt on the ironclad's port side has crumbled, while aft of the midships bulkhead there is other damage. Parts of the corroding hull have sagged or collapsed, and the only remaining section of the lower hull now is supported only by the *Monitor*'s boilers and steam machinery. With each expedition season, divers photograph hull plates that have slipped to the ocean floor or that dangle precariously from the wreck. In 1993, a NOAA-lead team verified that the turret's upturned wooden deck had disintegrated, allowing silt to fill the turret space. The deck section resting on the turret has split open due to the weight of the armored hull pressing into the turret.

Another complicating factor emerged in 1999, when navy divers confirmed what historians had documented: after the *Monitor*'s return to Hampton Roads before the sinking, a rifle shield that had not been part of John Ericsson's original design was attached to the turret. When new, it would have been about four feet high. A large portion of the shield remains, and together with the turret it bears the weight of the overlying hull section and internal machinery. The situation is tenuous because even a relatively small shift in the position of the hull could change the angle of force impinging on the turret and shield, perhaps triggering a break in the turret's iron wall. This sort of speculation makes it uncomfortably easy to conjure a scenario in which recovery of the intact "cheese box," symbol of a revolution in naval warfare, would suddenly become much more difficult, or even impossible. Another real threat is the total collapse of the *Monitor*'s corroded hull—a cataclysm that would damage or destroy many of the ironclad's innovative components and historic artifacts.

View of the turret, now almost filled with silt. A portion of the ironclad's armor belt is visible at the upper left. Courtesy Rod Farb.

The Challenges of Recovery

One factor working in the wreck's favor, however, is that the technology and know-how required to safely hoist major components of the ironclad upward through the sea is advancing. Even so, raising massive artifacts from the sea floor without destroying other recoverable parts requires personnel and equipment specialized for subsea rigging and lifting, and where the *Monitor* is concerned that apparatus will have to be capable of some heavy lifting: the ironclad's turret, built of 186 joined iron plates, weighs more than 240,000 pounds, and her engine and boiler system together weigh another 200,000 pounds. One of the biggest challenges in a *Monitor* recovery effort is determining how to get hold of and lift such heavy, bulky objects when they are so deep in the ocean. The U.S. Navy is assisting NOAA with the development of detailed plans for recovery of portions of the *Monitor.* Oceaneering International, Inc., the navy's salvage contractor, has to its credit the recovery of large pieces of TWA's Flight 800 aircraft, which crashed into the sea off the northeastern U.S. in 1996. In Oceaneering's estimation, the best method for recovery of major *Monitor* components will be "direct lift," using cranes and other heavy-lift equipment mounted on a vessel such as a derrick barge to bring components to the surface. The exact lift systems used may include custom-designed lifting frames, cages and baskets, custom spreader bars, and nylon or wire slings. At that point, the detailed documentation of the position and condition of the wreck's parts will enter the calculation, with recovery tools and techniques being customized to each artifact. Given the changeable conditions surrounding the wreck, some pieces of equipment will probably have to be fabricated or modified on site.

If time in the corrosive embrace of the ocean has been the *Monitor*'s enemy, time can be an equally formidable foe when an artifact is exposed

A crane lifts the Monitor's *propeller into a Mariners' Museum vehicle for transport to the museum, where the three-to-five-year process of conservation has begun.*
<small>Courtesy of The Mariners' Museum</small>

to air. Hence, before a small artifact is sent to the surface, it must be placed in a plastic bag and stored inside the diver's recovery box. At the surface, artifacts are photographed; small objects are then immersed in seawater in a preservation container, while larger ones are wrapped in plastic for transport to The Mariners' Museum, where long-term conservation of all the artifacts will take place.

Recovery work depends on taking advantage of patches of calm weather and quiet water. Such good times converged in early June 1998, when divers were able to saw through the shaft of the *Monitor*'s four-bladed, 4,600-pound propeller, rig a lifting bridle around it, and haul it via ship-mounted crane to the surface in a single, long diver-assisted lift. In an effort that had begun early in the morning, divers and ship-based navy and NOAA personnel worked

LEFT: *Glass bottles on the sea floor at the wreck site.* COURTESY OF BARB LANDER. ABOVE: *A crushed copper container that may have been an oil cup used by George Geer or another of the ship's crew.* FROM THE COLLECTIONS OF THE MARINER'S MUSEUM.

without letup nearly until midnight, when the propeller came aboard under a starry sky. Retrieving the propeller had been a priority because its angle of repose was seriously stressing the ironclad's stern. Today the nine-foot screw resides in a tank at The Mariners' Museum, wired with dozens of platinum-coated copper anodes and submerged in an electrolytic solution of water and sodium carbonate. A mild electric current runs through the metal, breaking up corrosive iron chlorides and forcing them to the outside. Conservation experts estimate that it will take at least three years of electrolysis to rid the propeller of its 136-year load of contaminants, so that it can be safely put on public display.

It is thrilling to retrieve large objects from the *Monitor* wreck, but expedition divers also are charged with bringing up small artifacts after each object's location has been recorded for posterity. In recent years such found treasures have run the gamut from objects from the captain's stateroom and china from the wardroom to lumps of coal, chunks of deck plating, and a slew of objects so encrusted with marine life that they will be unrecognizable until they also undergo conservation. Removing the blanket of marine life sometimes divulges surprises: an algae-encrusted mass of metal and pipe, originally thought to be one of the gallant little ironclad's innovative flush toilets, quickly was revealed to be a more prosaic component, either an intake or discharge valve that was part of the engine system. Hundreds of bolts with two-inch, wrought iron hex nuts were used

Now encrusted with coral and other marine life, this gauge was once part of the Monitor's *engine machinery.*
Courtesy Monitor National Marine Sanctuary (NOAA).

to fasten together the iron walls of the *Monitor's* gun turret, and one of them was recovered in 1998. When the NOAA team removed the nut and bolt using only a pipe wrench and their fingers, they all but cheered. The nut unscrewed cleanly, revealing shiny metal threads— not a crumbling mess as some conservators had feared.

⸱

Painstakingly, the archaeological surveys, measurements, and the assembly of vital engineering data have paved the way for final preparations for recovery of some of the most historically important parts of the ship. In 1998 NOAA established a clear direction for this endgame: shoring the hull; followed by recovery of the engine, part of the armor belt; and then, finally, recovery of the turret itself. Shoring is a low-tech but dynamic operation in which, as the changing situation demands, divers and engineers select from a menu of options including pumping sand into the open area beneath the hull, buttressing it with bags of sand or cement pumped from the surface.

With the hull shored, the portion of lower hull to which the engine is attached can be cut away, its support beams and iron plating recovered as part of the assembly. Then the entire assembly can be retrieved. The *Monitor*'s creator John Ericsson was a tinkerer; historical records indicate that he ordered various last-minute changes that, in the rush to build the ironclad, were never recorded. Recovering the engine and, subsequently, the associated auxiliary equipment will help fill in many of these small, intriguing details.

With the engine and other machinery out of the way, the hull section and armor belting that bar access to the turret can be cut away; like the lower hull already removed, they too will probably be recovered from the *Monitor* Sanctuary. Then the turret's contents will be carefully mapped and removed. Finally clear of obstructions, the turret and rifle shield will be ready for their last journey. A specially crafted cradle will be rigged around and under the turret, supporting it on all sides. Then a crane aboard a salvage ship, possibly a naval vessel, will slowly raise the turret to the surface. From there, the rescued *Monitor* artifacts will embark upon a new journey—expert conservation to insure long-term preservation, then into new quarters at The Mariners' Museum. There, alongside the letters of George S. Geer, they can tell their dramatic and poignant story for generations to come.

n as they liked
to eating the Offic
t Give my Love
d Kiss the Babys

Your Loving

George

NOTES

CHAPTER 1: THE DUEL

1. *Official Records of the Union and Confederate Navies in the War of the Rebellion*, 31 vols. (Washington, D.C.: Government Printing Office, 1894–1922), Series 1, 6:517. Hereafter, this source will be abbreviated as *ORN*, with all citations from Series 1 unless otherwise noted.

2. *Ibid.*; Samuel Dana Greene, "In the *Monitor* Turret," in Clarence C. Buel and Robert U. Johnson, eds., *Battles and Leaders of the Civil War*, 4 vols. (New York: Century, 1884–1888), 1:719.

3. At the Portsmouth Navy Yard about this time, prospective sailors were told that the "deadhead" time between enlistment and assignment to a ship would count toward their pay, but that handy incentive also proved inaccurate.

4. Declaration for Pension, Martha C. Geer Pension File, Certificate 9508, Approved Navy Dependent Pension Files (M-1279), National Archives [hereafter abbreviated NA].; Enlistment Returns, Changes, and Reports, 1846–1942, Entry 224, Navy Department Files, RD 24, NA.

5. See the plan of the berth deck in John Ericsson, "The Building of the *Monitor*," in *Battles and Leaders of the Civil War*, 1:735; Robert W. Daly, ed., *Aboard the USS* Monitor, *1862: The Letters of Acting Paymaster William Frederick Keeler* (Annapolis, Md.: Naval Institute Press, 1964), 20, 56.

6. ORN, 6:659, 669–70, 676; Daly, *Aboard the USS* Monitor, 18–19.

7. ORN, 6:672, 679, 681, 682, 683.

8. *Ibid.*, 6:684; Daly, *Aboard the USS* Monitor, 27–31; Alban C. Stimers, "An Engineer Aboard the *Monitor*," *Civil War Times Illustrated* 9:1 (April 1970), 29–30; Greene, "In the *Monitor* Turret," 720–21.

9. ORN, 7:8–11, 18–24, 44–46.

10. Greene, "In the *Monitor* Turret," 721–22; Daly, *Aboard the USS* Monitor, 31–32, 40.

11. Greene, "In the *Monitor* Turret," 722–23; Stimers, "An Engineer Aboard the *Monitor*," 32–33; Daly, *Aboard the USS* Monitor, 34–35, 40; ORN, 7:27.

12. Stimers, "An Engineer Aboard the *Monitor*," 33, 35; ORN, 7:25–27; Daly, *Aboard the USS* Monitor, 37, 39, 64; Greene, "In the *Monitor* Turret," 725–27.

13. Greene, "In the *Monitor* Turret," 726–27; ORN, 7:26–27; Daly, *Aboard the USS* Monitor, 38–39.

CHAPTER 2: THE STANDOFF

1. Daly, *Aboard the USS* Monitor, 43, 55.

2. *War of the Rebellion: Official Records of the Union and Confederate Armies*, 128 vols. (Washington, D.C.: Government Printing Office, 1880–1901), Series 1, 9:27, 30. Hereafter OR, with all citations from Series 1 unless otherwise noted; Stimers, "An Engineer Aboard the *Monitor*," 35.

3. ORN, 7:98; Daly, *Aboard the USS* Monitor, 53, 55.

4. Daly, *Aboard the USS* Monitor, 69. Geer confused the days of the week when he told Martha about this latest visiting general, mistaking the day of his arrival at Fort Monroe for Thursday and his jaunt to the ironclad as Friday. Paymaster Keeler recorded that Little Mac arrived during the dinner hour on Thursday, April 3; McClellan could not have made a late afternoon visit to the ship after that day; he started up the peninsula toward Yorktown on Friday, April 4, and by 8:30 P.M. had advanced his headquarters as far as Big Bethel, about a dozen miles from Fort Monroe.

5. Stephen W. Sears, *The Civil War Papers of George B. McClellan* (New York: Ticknor & Fields, 1989), 225–28; OR, 11 (Part 1):296, 299, 300–5.

6. ORN, 7:223–24

7. OR, 11 (Part 1):367

8. Daly, *Aboard the USS* Monitor, 84–85.

9. ORN, 7:39–40, 276, 705, and Series 2, 1:90

CHAPTER 3: THE RIVER

1. OR, 11 (Part 3):497; David Donald, ed., *Inside Lincoln's Cabinet: The Civil War Diaries of Salmon P. Chase* (New York: Longmans, Green, 1954), 76–77; Daly, *Aboard the USS* Monitor, 107; ORN, 7:326.

2. Donald, *Inside Lincoln's Cabinet*, 78–79; ORN, 7:335–36, 338.

3. ORN, 7:336–37, 340; OR, 11 (Part 1):634.

4. Daly, *Aboard the USS* Monitor, 123–26.

5. *Ibid.*, 126; ORN, 7:352–55, 357–58, 362, 410–11.

6. ORN, 7:394–99, 734; OR, 11 (Part 1):640–41; Daly, *Aboard the USS* Monitor, 133–35.

CHAPTER 4: INTERLUDE

1. Daly, *Aboard the USS* Monitor, 153.

2. ORN, 7:444, 450.

3. Daly, *Aboard the USS* Monitor, 158.

4. *Ibid.*, 21–22.

5. ORN, 7:493–94.

6. ORN, 7:477, 491–92, 495; OR, 11 (Part 3):250.

CHAPTER 5: THE RETREAT

1. Sears, Steven W., *To the Gates of Richmond* (New York: Ticknor & Fields, 1992), 222–49.

2. Daly, *Aboard the USS* Monitor, 165–70; ORN, 7:524; OR, 11 (Part 3):623.

3. ORN, 7:532–34.

4. Clifford Dowdey, ed., *The Wartime Papers of R. E. Lee* (New York: Bramhall House, 1961), 208; ORN, 7:542.

5. ORN, 7:60–61, 543–46; Daly, *Aboard the USS* Monitor, 182–85.
6. ORN, 7:571.
7. OR, Series 3, 2:280–82.

CHAPTER 6: THE LANDING

1. Daly, *Aboard the USS* Monitor, 158.
2. *Ibid.*, 182.
3. OR, 11 (Part 3):337.
4. *Ibid.*, 337–38; Daniel Reed Larned to "My Dear Sister, July 21, [25], 1862," Daniel Reed Larned Papers, Library of Congress.
5. Daly, *Aboard the USS* Monitor, 198, 205; ORN, 7:599.
6. ORN, 7:589–90, 633.
7. Daly, *Aboard the USS* Monitor, 197–98.
8. *Ibid.*, 198.
9. OR, 11 (Part 1):76, and 11 (Part 2):941–42; ORN, 7:607; Daly, *Aboard the USS* Monitor, 199, 203.
10. OR, 11 (Part 1):77–78, 80–82; Daly, *Aboard the USS* Monitor, 202; ORN, 7:62931.
11. Dowdey, *The Wartime Papers of R. E. Lee*, 246–47.
12. OR, 11 (Part 3):372–73.
13. OR, 11 (Part 3):376–77, 675–76; Daly, *Aboard the USS* Monitor, 208.
14. Daly, *Aboard the USS* Monitor, 209.

CHAPTER 7: NEWPORT NEWS

1. Daly, *Aboard the USS* Monitor, 209, 210; ORN, 7:654.
2. Daly, *Aboard the USS* Monitor, 217.
3. *Ibid.*, 212.
4. ORN, 7:686, 688; Daly, *Aboard the USS* Monitor, 212–13.
5. Daly, *Aboard the USS* Monitor, 216. Both Paymaster Keeler and Geer referred to Daniel Moore as the wardroom steward, but Moore was the officers' cook at this point, while the steward served as a general servant to the wardroom. Moore appears to have been demoted to steward in November, unless he performed alternating duties. Moore went down with the *Monitor* four months later.

6. Daly, *Aboard the USS* Monitor, 219.

7. OR, 2:438–39, and 19 (Part 1):799–800.

8. OR, 2:52, 53, 294–96. This site lies on The Mariners' Museum property, where Geer's letters reside.

9. On the same day that Geer visited the burned-out neighborhood, Paymaster Keeler recorded Commander Bankhead's flattering comments about McClellan. Daly, *Aboard the USS* Monitor, 219.

10. *Ibid.,* 225.

CHAPTER 8: WASHINGTON

1. Daly, *Aboard the USS* Monitor, 226–28.

2. OR, Series 3, 2:645, 663, 666–69, 881.

3. *Troy (N.Y.) Record,* March 10, 1922; *New York Times,* December 4, 1938.

4. Daly, *Aboard the USS* Monitor, 229–30.

5. Robert Means Thompson and Richard Wainwright, eds., *Confidential Correspondence of Gustavus Vasa Fox, Assistant Secretary of the Navy, 1861–1865,* 2 vols. (New York: Naval Historical Society, 1919–1920), 2:165.

6. Daly, *Aboard the USS* Monitor, 236.

CHAPTER 9: THE CAROLINA SHORE

1. *ORN,* 8:298, 317.

2. Daly, *Aboard the USS* Monitor, 248–49; *ORN,* 8:317.

3. Daly, *Aboard the USS* Monitor, 249–50.

4. See Geer's letter to his brother of January 13, 1863.

5. *ORN,* 7:341, 342, and 8:332, 368, 369, 377.

6. *ORN,* 8:326–27, 331, and Series 2, 1:149.

7. *ORN,* 8:329, 337, 350; OR, 18:495–96.

8. *ORN,* 8:347, 349–50. Geer's letter to his brother Gilbert of January 13, 1863, tends to give him a more central role in the drama, claiming that he communicated directly with Bankhead. Official reports written within two days of the sinking suggest otherwise.

9. *ORN,* 8:347–48; Francis B. Butts, "The Loss of the *Monitor,*" in Clarence C. Buel and Robert U. Johnson, eds., *Battles and Leaders of the Civil War,* 4 vols. (New York: Century, 1884–1888), 1:745; Daly, *Aboard the USS* Monitor, 256.

Butts, who had only signed on as a landsman at Washington in November, also recalled himself as a prominent character in the sinking of his ship, and his recollections bear judicious reading. His memory, at least, did not prove flawless, as he mistook both the time of the *Monitor*'s departure from Hampton Roads and its intended destination.

10. *ORN*, 8:348, 350.

11. *ORN*, 8:340, 348, 351, 356; Butts, "The Loss of the *Monitor*," 746.

12. *ORN*, 8:354.

13. *Ibid.*, 341–42.

14. *ORN*, 8:354.

15. A navy clerk's 1893 endorsement in Martha Geer's pension file holds that Geer was appointed January 19, 1863, and reported on the *Galena* that same day, but the letters contradict that. The appointment and orders would have been signed in Washington, and would have been delivered through channels, taking several days to reach him. See Martha C. Geer Pension File, NA.

BIBLIOGRAPHY

MANUSCRIPTS

Enlistment Returns, Changes, and Reports, 1846–1942, Entry 224, Navy
     Department Files, RG 24. National Archives, Washington, D.C.
Larned, Daniel Reed. Papers. Library of Congress, Washington, D.C.
Martha C. Geer Pension File, Certificate 9508, Approved Navy Dependents
     Pension Files (M-1279). National Archives, Washington, D.C.
Tenth Census of the United States (T-9). National Archives, Washington, D.C.

PUBLISHED WORKS

Butts, Francis B. "The Loss of the 'Monitor,'" Clarence C. Buel and Robert U.
     Johnson, eds., *Battles and Leaders of the Civil War,* 4 vols. New York: The
     Century Co., 1884–1888.
Daly, Robert W., ed. *Aboard the USS* Monitor, *1862: The Letters of Acting Paymaster
     William Frederick Keeler.* Annapolis, Md.: Naval Institute Press, 1964.

Donald, David, ed. *Inside Lincoln's Cabinet: The Civil War Diaries of Salmon P. Chase.* New York: Longmans, Green & Co., 1954.

Dowdey, Clifford, ed. *The Wartime Papers of R. E. Lee.* New York: Bramhall House, 1961.

Ericsson, John. "The Building of the 'Monitor,'" Clarence C. Buel and Robert U. Johnson, eds., *Battles and Leaders of the Civil War,* 4 vols. New York: The Century Co., 1884–1888.

Greene, Samuel Dana. "In the 'Monitor' Turret," Clarence C. Buel and Robert U. Johnson, eds., *Battles and Leaders of the Civil War,* 4 Vols. New York: The Century Co., 1884–1888.

Hubinger, Bert. "A Visit to the *Monitor,*" *Civil War Times Illustrated* (June, 1997).

———. "Can We Raise the *Monitor?,*" *Civil War Times Illustrated* (June, 1997).

McClellan, George B. *McClellan's Own Story.* New York: Charles L. Webster & Co., 1887.

Official Records of the Union and Confederate Navies in the War of the Rebellion, 31 vols. Washington, D.C.: Government Printing Office, 1894–1922.

Sears, Stephen W. *The Civil War Papers of George B. McClellan.* New York: Ticknor & Fields, 1989.

———. *To the Gates of Richmond.* New York: Ticknor & Fields, 1992.

Stimers, Alban C. "An Engineer Aboard the *Monitor,*" *Civil War Times Illustrated* (April, 1970).

Thompson, Robert Means, and Richard Wainwright, eds. *Confidential Correspondence of Gustavus Vasa Fox, Assistant Secretary of the Navy, 1861–1865,* 2 vols. New York: The Naval Historical Society, 1919–1920.

War of the Rebellion: Official Records of the Union and Confederate Armies, 128 vols. Washington, D.C.: Government Printing Office, 1880–1901.

NEWSPAPERS

The New York Times.
Troy (N.Y.) Record.

INDEX

Page numbers in *italics* refer to illustrations.

Norfolk Public Library

0 1186 0764069 5

NO LONGER ~~THE PROPERTY~~ OF
LITTLE CREEK BRANCH
NORFOLK PUBLIC LIBRARY

OCT 09 2003

DEMCO